MAN thinks in MENTAL PICTURES, not in words. Associated with every MENTAL IMAGE of a LIFE EXPERIENCE is the FEELING Man had at the time. Each individual, today, is the SUM TOTAL of his MENTAL and EMOTIONAL REACTION to whatever has happened to him, up to the present moment.

What he is—is represented by the MENTAL IMAGE he has of himself and his ATTITUDE toward LIFE and OTHERS.

Man is DOMINATED, then, at any given moment by what he THINKS and how he FEELS.

Reduced to utter simplicity—if an individual thinks GOOD thoughts—he will eventually attract GOOD things.

Harold Sherman

Fawcett Books
by Harold Sherman:

HOW TO FORESEE AND CONTROL YOUR FUTURE

HOW TO KNOW WHAT TO BELIEVE

HOW TO MAKE ESP WORK FOR YOU

HOW TO PICTURE WHAT YOU WANT

HOW TO TAKE YOURSELF APART AND PUT
YOURSELF TOGETHER AGAIN

THOUGHTS THROUGH SPACE (with Sir Hubert Wilkins)

KNOW YOUR OWN MIND

YOU CAN COMMUNICATE WITH THE UNSEEN WORLD

YOU LIVE AFTER DEATH

YOUR KEY TO HAPPINESS

YOUR POWER TO HEAL

HOW TO
PICTURE WHAT
YOU WANT

———

Harold Sherman

A FAWCETT GOLD MEDAL BOOK • NEW YORK

The author and publisher are grateful for permission to reprint the following:

Excerpts from "What Do We Really Know About Psychic Phenomena?"
By Laile E. Bartlett, Reader's Digest, August 1977.

"Some Enchanted Evening" from SOUTH PACIFIC. Copyright © 1949 by Richard Rodgers & Oscar Hammerstein II. Copyright renewed/Williamson Music, Inc., owner of publication & allied rights throughout the Western Hemisphere & Japan. International Copyright secured/ALL RIGHTS RESERVED/Used by permission.

From To Kiss Earth Goodbye by Ingo Swann. Copyright © 1975 by Ingo Swann. By permission of Hawthorn Books, Inc.

From Psychic News, August, 1977, article on Dr. Elizabeth Kubler-Ross. By permission of Psychic News, 23 Great Queen Street, London WC2B 5BB.

HOW TO PICTURE WHAT YOU WANT

Published by Fawcett Gold Medal Books, a unit of CBS Publications, the Consumer Publishing Division of CBS Inc.

ISBN: 0-449-14003-2

Printed in the United States of America

10 9 8 7 6 5 4 3 2 1

CONTENTS

*Dedicated With Love and
Profound Admiration
To
HARRY and CAPPY MORGAN,
President and Executive
Director, respectively,
of Friendship Ambassadors
New York City, whose
"people-to-people" cultural
and educational exchange
programs are touching the
minds and hearts of Young
People throughout the world.*

CHAPTER 1

—————————————

The Present World You Live In

You are a far greater person than you have ever thought yourself to be. Regardless of your time of life, the kind of body or mind with which you came into this world or have developed, the experiences you have had to date—good and bad—Science is now joining with Religion to produce evidence that every human creature possesses, whether he realizes it or not, unlimited possibilities for development beyond his most fantastic dreams.

Hard to believe? Of course it is! Right now, as you look back over your life and scan the world around you, it may seem that most of humanity is in a mess, perhaps including yourself. You may be worried about your health or that of a friend or loved one; or your economic condition; or your marital status; or the conduct of your children; or people you can't get along with; or someone who has taken advantage of you; or the increasing threat of droughts, earthquakes, tornadoes, floods; pollution of air and water and land and food from pesticides, additives and radiation—not to mention the possibility of World War Three—all indications of the unstable state of things on this planet! You are finding yourself alive at a time when the "have" and "have-not" nations in this world are in the midst of violent change.

You feel that much that is happening is beyond your control. In most communities, big and small, it isn't safe to be out after dark; muggings, robberies, and murders are taking place in areas once considered safe. You hear stories of wife beatings, child abuse, of record divorce rates, of millions living without benefit of wedlock, of dishonesty in high places and low, of widespread rape, of gangsterlike murders, bombings, skyjackings, political assassinations, and all manner of criminal assaults on what remains of so-called decent Society.

So how can you enjoy any feelings of security, any assurance of happiness, or maintain the faith in God you once had? Something is basically, terribly wrong. You are on an island surrounded by turmoil and uncertainty . . . things aren't what they were only a few short years ago. There is danger of a fuel shortage, when gas and oil will be severely rationed, and when there may not be enough gas and coal and electricity for heating—and if there is, can most people afford to buy it? You hear of the coming Age of Solar Energy and the need for greater insulation of homes and offices—all of which costs money. How can you face what is coming on a limited income, already depleted by inflation?

Where can you go? What can you do to escape this horrendous series of critical events which appears to be looming on the horizon? Any one of a number of these developments would be bad enough if you found yourself in the way of their happening.

My wife Martha and I have friends who have bought property in a barren part of a western state, thirty miles from any habitation. They actually intend to build a little home with an air-raid and radiation-free shelter, a generator to supply power, a deep well for water, a quantity of dry food, and intend to sit out whatever comes. They do not think they can be of any service in trying to help save the world, or even their next-door neighbors. They have decided it will be a full-time job saving themselves. This is the *image* they are carrying in their minds of the future—and since there is a great law of mind that "like always attracts like," they may be among the first to meet the very fate they are trying to avoid.

Of course, a big city isn't exactly the safest place to be in if any major catastrophe should occur, but few of us are able to run away—even if we could. We might far better take counsel with ourselves and decide that the wisest approach is to prepare ourselves physically, mentally, emotionally, and spiritually for whatever is to come!

This simply means that, as we view the "life scene" around us, it should become increasingly obvious that the answer to personal and world problems has to lie, to a great degree, within ourselves!

The *thrust* of what I will have to say to you, as we discuss this situation together, is contained in the evidence I intend to present. As I stated at the outset, that you are greater than you know. You have a Higher Power within your consciousness upon which you can learn to rely—that, properly directed, can take you from where you are to where you want to be. It can give you guidance and protection. It can help you overcome your fears and give you the courage and the faith to stand up under whatever may happen. In short, it can enable you to make your own world—and live in it!

How is this possible?

I have repeated, time and again, in my series of self-help books, such as *How to Make ESP Work for You*, *How to Foresee and Control Your Future*, and *Your Key to Happiness*, a description of how the mind operates—knowledge that is not original with me, which even the ancients understood, but ways of thinking which I have been able to prove and demonstrate in my more than sixty years of research and personal experimentation.

These laws of mind, once put in motion by right thinking, will work for you as effectively as they have worked for me and thousands of others. Perhaps, to a degree, you are already aware of these higher powers, but it is safe to assume that you have not begun to realize their greater potential in your life. Nobody has!

Start by recognizing that the External World, as you see it today, is pretty much the product of man's thought. You have made your small contribution to it by the way you have reacted and are reacting to the things that have happened or are happening to you because everyone's thoughts and feelings, magnified by the BILLIONS now on earth, are having a definite, interrelated influence on the shaping of the earth's destiny!

In other words—everything happens in MIND before it can happen in this Outer World. Your thoughts today are constantly helping create your future! Good *and* bad! You can't get away from it. While there is much we still do not know about the mysteries of our own minds, one fact has been established beyond all doubt. It doesn't matter what race or color or religion, or knowledge or education—intelligent or ignorant, primitive or advanced in world knowledge, everyone's mind functions basically the same way!

Here, in brief outline, is the undeniable, easily demonstrable PROOF!

MAN thinks in MENTAL PICTURES, not in words. Associated with every MENTAL IMAGE of a LIFE EXPERIENCE, is the FEELING Man had at the time— all recorded in Consciousness. Each individual, today, is the SUM TOTAL of his MENTAL and EMOTIONAL REACTION to whatever has happened to him, up to the present moment.

What he is is represented by the MENTAL IMAGE he has of himself, his ATTITUDE toward LIFE and OTHERS.

Man is DOMINATED, then, at any given moment by what he THINKS and how he FEELS.

Before Man can progress, he must realize that THOUGHT is a MIGHTY CREATIVE FORCE. Each thought, therefore, ACTIVATED by STRONG FEELINGS of FEAR or DESIRE, is a CREATIVE ACT which seeks to EXTERNALIZE itself in the form of some EXPERIENCE, constructive or destructive.

There is a UNIVERSAL LAW OF MIND that LIKE ALWAYS ATTRACTS LIKE.

Reduced to utter simplicity: if an individual thinks GOOD thoughts, he will eventually attract GOOD things; if he thinks BAD thoughts, he will ultimately attract BAD things.

What Every Man Needs to Know

Until Mankind is properly informed and shown the mechanics of mind operation, human creatures will continue to make wrong use of mind through wrong thinking and will bring greater and greater destruction upon themselves

The great tragedy of life on this planet is that man has filled his mind with knowledge of the world about him, but knows very little about the machinery of his own Consciousness. Consequently, he has permitted destructive feelings of hate, prejudice, greed, fear, lust for power, and like emotions to turn his creative forces against himself and others.

The religions of the world have sought to teach Man these TRUTHS, but Man has not been sufficiently impressed with his INDIVIDUAL RESPONSIBILITY for his own THOUGHTS and ACTS.

It has not been spelled out to him, beyond dogmas and creeds, in an impersonal and objective way, that Man, as a creature of free will and free choice, is largely the CREATOR of his own DESTINY. As such, he has been punishing himself by his own WRONG THINKING, rather than having been the victim of circumstances and feelings seemingly beyond his control.

These are realistic facts, simply stated, with which, like

it or not, you must be prepared to deal. Refusal to face the truths about yourself and the world about you will keep you from achieving the success and happiness and health you might otherwise enjoy.

There is great power in what I call PICTURIZA-TION—carrying an IMAGE in your mind of what you want to do or be or have . . . seeing yourself, in your mind's eye, *doing* it . . . or *being* it . . . or *having* it— as though it had *already* happened. These images set magnetic forces into action which begin attracting to you what you have visualized.

When I first described these powers and the technique for using them in 1935, in my book *Your Key to Happiness*, it was considered "pioneering," but now there is an explosion of public interest in the Mind and its unlimited possibilities. Much is being written about it and, I am sorry to say, there is a great deal of Science Fiction —many promises of achievement through Mind Control Methods which, however alluring, will not produce the results desired.

For example: such eye-catching statements in promotional material as "You can secretly command other people to do your bidding . . . you can direct the thoughts and acts of others without their knowing it . . . no matter how much they may not want to follow your commands, they will carry them out exactly as you wish. No one will have the faintest idea you are behind it. You alone know the secret powers you are using to get what you want in life."

Sounds great, doesn't it? "Within 3 minutes," the ads say, "you can begin turning on the power and watch others around you drop everything and do what they're told."

Well, I might as well tell you at the start that I cannot match these promises. But I can assure you that when you have gained a simple knowledge and control of your MENTAL IMAGERY—which is the CRUX of your entire thinking process—you can impress others favorably without trying to compel them to like you or do your bidding—and that you will be able to attract whatever is good for you and eliminate much that is not good, in and around you.

The great Victor Hugo once said, "Nothing in this world is so powerful as an IDEA whose time has come!"

The time of all times has come for you to make every-day use of the mighty power of PICTURIZATION! It is the greatest IDEA in the world!

CHAPTER 2

All Existence Starts with Imagery

Every form of life, everything in Nature starts with a pattern, a design, an image of what it is one day to be. Each seed contains a blueprint for its creative power within to follow when the environmental conditions are provided for it to emerge from its dormant state into manifestation.

Science now knows that all life—all physical form—emerges first from a gaseous state. The planets, the suns, the galaxies, all first existed in a gigantic gaseous state, beyond the capacity of our minds to conceive. If we could be projected into boundless space and view, at close range, a seemingly unlimited gaseous cloud, filled with all the elements and many more we have come to recognize today, we would observe the unthinkably great Creator at work!

Millions, even billions of years, as we have learned to count Time, have been required to produce our tiny speck of earth in the mighty cosmos, and our distant family of other planets, which we are now, at last, trying to reach, photograph, and land upon.

Try to imagine—because it is true—that there is order in the seeming chaos of fiery, gaseous explosions. The spirit of Creation is moving in and through it all. Colossal forces are shaping worlds to come and the myriads of life forms upon them.

How Creation started—if it ever did start as we can conceive of Time—is beyond human comprehension. All we know is that Creation is constantly taking place throughout a Timeless and Spaceless universe, and that we are now for the fleetingest of moments, ALIVE in it!

Why we came into existence here, rather than on any one of countless planets, is also a mystery that we will never solve—in this lifetime, at least. Why we entered existence as humans rather than as dogs or cats or whales or other forms of life that can be imagined, is another mystery.

Should we speculate that the universe is filled with limitless particles of pure intelligence awaiting magnetic attraction into swirling conglomerations of molecules which are to settle on some planet and evolve into physical shapes through which to manifest? Is this the way that the unthinkably Great Intelligence divides itself up and expands into countless forms of expression, adaptive to the needs of each developing environment?

And do we bear an affinity on subconscious levels for every other form of life? And have we emerged from an amoebalike start, passing up through a line of evolving life-forms until we have reached the human creature level? Have our direct ancestors passed on to us the essence of what they achieved physically and mentally through their experiences, on which we can instinctively draw as we face experiences of our own?

And are we destined to slip out of our earthly envelopes when the change called Death occurs, like a butterfly slipping out of a cocoon into a New Dimension—invisible to us here but no less real—with a higher-vibrating body form and an environment prepared for our existence there as this earth and its atmosphere has given us life here?

These are questions we may seldom ask ourselves. We just accept the fact that we exist on this planet, involved as we are with the business of living—its joys and sorrows, its ups and downs, its stresses and strains, its struggles and pains, its fears and worries, its disappointments and disillusionments, its sexual and romantic adventures, its wonders and tragedies, its good and evil moments, its everything that we call life and living. We give little thought to why we are here or where we are going, if anywhere, after we leave our residence in this wonderful physical body!

Well, these wonderings may or may not have any scientific validity, but I feel they are worth meditating upon as we try to get a deeper, more satisfying sense of who and what we are, the creative forces we possess, and how we can better understand and control and direct them in our journey through life on this planet.

Every form of life possesses what is required to exist in its element. It can function only within the limitations permitted by its organism.

Only Man has evolved a brain with the capacity to permit the life force in us to develop a Self-Awareness, a feeling of Identity, an "I am I" Consciousness—the sensing that it is a part of something greater than it is— a creative power which, rightly used, can lift Man to supreme heights, at times—or destroy him if it is wrongly used.

Question: Is this Life Force in us any different than the Life Force in any other form of life, except that, in the human body, it has a more refined instrument to manifest through? Would this Life Force or Intelligence in a dog or a cat, for example, transferred to a human organism, be able to develop and express on a human level with equal facility? Who knows?

All animals are concreted in Man. No hyena is so treacherous, no tiger so ferocious, no hog so brutish, no weasel so destructive, no animal creature of any sort is so perfect in its own peculiar nature as is the man who suffers any or all of these animal characteristics within him to run riot; and this is because his human soul or spirit is enslaved to the animal. Directed, guided by will, it ceases to be animal.

Is it possible that life has evolved in similar ways on all other planets—untold trillions, beyond conception? Has the species that is Man had to come up through lower forms in like environments? Or are conditions so different on many planets that totally different chemical combinations have permitted much higher manifestations of Intelligence?

And what of our concept of God in a universe we now realize is so vast that life comparable to or surpassing ours must exist on many planets? Must we not consider intelligent beings wherever they are to be found, still children of the same God or Creator?

What does this increasing awareness of life throughout this boundless universe do to all our religions on earth? Certainly our reason tells us that inhabitants of other planets will not have been exposed to our ways of thinking or feel the need for a crucified Savior, an only Son of God, dying to save them from their sins, or to assure them of immortal life.

We have historic evidence of spiritual leaders like Confucius, Lao Tse, Buddha, Mohammed, and Jesus who have left their mark on the consciousness of millions down to the present day.

Man has sought to explain his existence here and to image a godlike Being or Creator responsible for it all whom he could worship and to whom he could offer sacrifices and ask for help, forgiveness and guidance. Millions have died for their beliefs or been killed for their beliefs throughout all history on this planet. This fearsome clinging to the faiths of their fathers is still continuing.

Not until Mankind changes the images of its gods can it free itself from its savage hatreds and racial and religious prejudices brought about by misguided spiritual thinking. As I intend to point out again and again, we must realize that the images we carry in our minds have a profound effect on everything we think and do, as well as our attitudes toward others.

In the days when human creatures thought that this earth was the center of the universe, that everything revolved around us, that this planet was created for man's exclusive abode by a vengeful and jealous God who punished us by flood and fire and earthquake, and even pestilences, for our wrongdoings, we tried in every way to placate our Creator, to protect us from misfortune, and to assure us of favors in the sight of God.

Those days are still with us with some peoples. Wrong or false images, deeply embedded through years of worshipful thinking, resist removal, largely due to fear and ignorance.

The coming of the Space Age has drastically changed our IMAGE of the world around us and within us. We, as human creatures, can never be the same again. We cannot feel secure about our religious faith or our economic stability or our relationship between peoples of other countries, or even our next-door neighbors.

Our former images of our planet earth and our residence upon it have been shattered. We are having a difficult time trying to hold on to the image of a world which exists no longer. Often these past images have brought us feelings of security and satisfaction, and we dislike having to let go of them, to form new, realistic images of the world as it exists today.

Many present-day images are not very happy ones—and we find ourselves resisting the thought of having to live with them. We don't like to PICTURE what we may have to face as we see these world changes coming closer and closer to impinging upon our personal lives and favored ways of living.

Science is already looking ahead toward a time when this small planet will be overpopulated—when great numbers of us will have to seek refuge by colonizing some other livable planet, if one can be found and prepared for our coming. Fantastic? Buck Rogerish? It's already on the drawing boards!

And there are increasing indications that dwellers on other planets may have visited our earth centuries ago, brought life here, and possibly cohabited with some of our early ancestors! There is speculation that the current UFOs may be bringing some of these intelligent beings back, who have looked in on us before. Some of us hope that they are returning for a protective rather than hostile purpose, to help us out of our self-created troubles perhaps even save us from atomically destroying ourselves!

These are thoughts that may or may not be new to you, but they are going to crowd in on your consciousness sooner or later because they are destined to relate to your existence here and the new experiences that are headed your way.

Do you think you are ready to change your IMAGERY—to attempt to see life as it is today—to prepare to meet what is to come—to get your mental house in order so that you can begin picturing what you have to do to protect yourself and loved ones and to create a new kind of happiness and security in this disturbed world?

This is what this book is all about. It is what this life is all about. A great scientist once said, "The only thing permanent in the universe is CHANGE!"

This is true, and we must learn to live with CHANGE! You don't have to be upset by it, you can learn to ride with it! And you need not fear to change your concepts of your Creator because the Supreme Intelligence which is behind this magnificent universe is closer to you than you may now realize. In fact, it is my conviction that a part of God, the Great Intelligence—dwells within our Consciousness and we are MINIATURE CO-CREATORS with Him of our life here and the ever-unfolding life to come in Dimensions beyond our imagination!

When you carry this IMAGE in your Consciousness, nothing can basically harm you. Regardless of what may happen in this Outer World, you will inwardly know that all will be well with you and yours!

CHAPTER 3

The Influence of Childhood Imagery

To a great extent, man's conduct and behavior is ruled by how he thinks about himself and others.

He comes into this life knowing nothing. His mind is a blank page waiting to be written upon by the experiences he will have. As a baby he is helpless, dependent on the care and protection of his elders; those who have been in life before him, usually his mother and father.

As he enters more and more into life, his past experiences are recorded in imagery form in his Subconscious. The lessons they have taught him of what to do or not to do, give him feedback guidance as he faces new, untried experiences. Should he do a thing or not do it? What does a similar past experience tell him? What information does his memory bank report to him? Should he act on what he feels is right or wrong based on past experience, or should he venture on a new course of thought or action?

His baby mind is spongelike in its reaching out to absorb knowledge from its expanding environment and the influence of all life around him. Long before he can express his feelings in words, he is learning through feeling, and these feelings form images of the world in which he finds himself.

It has been said: "Give me a child for the first seven years of his life, and I care not who tries to influence him after that time."

There is considerable truth to this declaration because the child mind is extremely sensitive and impressionable. It has no developed reasoning faculty to weigh or evaluate the experiences which are mostly wished or forced upon it. It usually accepts them without resistance and begins to act in accordance with the nature of these thoughts and feelings.

We know now that sexual feelings and habits are formed early in life as a child becomes acquainted with his or her body. Young boys and girls have no awareness of right or wrong from a moral sense. They just react or respond as they feel and the images of whatever they do or is done to them, if these experiences have brought pleasure, become rooted in consciousness with the desire to be repeated as opportunity permits.

As a child grows older and parents or others observe tendencies which they look upon as abnormal or harmful, the child is punished or rebuked without too much understanding or explanation of the WHY, which causes the child to attempt to repress these thoughts and feelings. In this way, guilt and sinful concepts are introduced to the child mind. He may also develop, at this time, religious conflicts which can traumatically affect his attitude toward his own and the opposite sex for life.

IMAGERY! Its wrong or misguided implantation—the damage it can cause—the many ruined lives which can be attributed to it!

No one of us can escape the bombardment of images, good and bad, enticing or revolting, coming to us from every medium of communication and resulting from every experience that we have because, I'm going to repeat this again and again so you will never forget it—we think basically in PICTURES! Our consciousness is filled with them—and what we think, and feel, at any time of life, we ARE!

Today the average child mind is in danger of corruption before it is old enough to protect itself or know better. Economic need takes millions of mothers away from home long hours each day, trying to help earn a living. Young ones are left to baby-sitters, many of whom are incapable and even dissolute. They govern the children left in their charge by various forms of punishment and malevolent suggestions. If baby-sitters entertain boyfriends in the home, and many do, their conduct may not always be of the kind to which children should be exposed; and baby-sitters themselves may not be averse to seducing a child or children to different sex practices.

In these high-pressure times, many fathers and mothers are not mentally and emotionally stable and are disposed to take out their pent-up feelings on their children, who are already sensitively upset by their parents' ill behavior toward each other. We hear now of millions of battered babies and young ones who are often left alone for hours, locked in homes and apartments, suffering from malnutrition and serious injuries.

As if this is not bad enough, we are getting more and more evidence of widespread incestuous relations entered in by parents and relatives with their children.

Think of the mental images, with the powerfully associated feeling reactions which such abused children are carrying in their Consciousness! Most of them feel unwanted and rejected, are lacking in incentive to do anything but defend themselves as best they can and hide and stay out of the way.

Add to this the staggering divorce problem, the separation of mothers and fathers, the tug of war for the custody of children, the attempt to use children as pawns in making settlements, and the hate instead of love expressed between all parties. Consider what this does to the minds of all concerned and the unhappy, tragic IMAGES with which everyone—especially the children—have to cope!

With more than ten million alcoholics—men and women—in this country alone, and uncounted more addicted to some form of dope, the resulting broken and battered homes, the children are again caught in the middle of a bruising, unloving, soul-shattering experience. Are they to be blamed if this sorry example does not drive a sizable percentage into excessive drinkers and users of dope?

The only recourse for many is to run away from home in the desperate hope of finding or making a better way of life for themselves. But waiting around the corner to take advantage of their juvenile misery with offers of feigned sympathy and often tempting economic support are drug pushers and sex-perverted pornography and prostitution traffickers who manage to induce a goodly number to lend the use of their bodies in various ways for a price.

Do you now wonder that any child in today's world grows to adulthood unscarred? When a young person is surfeited with mental images of perverted conduct on all sides; when he sees motion pictures in theaters and on TV screens, spelling out in lurid, naked detail the joys of drinking and sexual carousing; when he is surrounded by kids his own age, as well as elders, who are doing it—he begins to wonder if he isn't missing something, if these practices do not represent the normal—almost the accepted!

Remember, I have said: "Like attracts like in the realm of mind"—a fact I will also reiterate time and again, since this infallible law of mind has a fundamental bearing on everything that happens to you in life.

When a young person or anyone lives with mental images of sexual practices, his own sexual desires cannot help being stimulated. He may repress them for a time, but the more he sees himself as a participant rather than an observer, the more this creative power of mind is impelled or ordered to begin magnetically attracting opportunities for indulgence. Ultimately there comes a breakpoint, and once the first step is taken, other sexual adventures become easier and easier, especially if the first experience has proved to be erotically satisfying.

To further elucidate: If a child has had his first sexual experience through seduction by an older person of the same sex and finds it to have been pleasurable despite being possibly shocking, he will tend to remember it, to reflect upon it, to fantasize having another experience of a similar nature, and, if approached again, he may be receptive to a repetition.

When such a child widens his sexual experience by having intercourse with a member or members of the opposite sex, he then tends to compare his memory of the pleasure he derived from the homosexual act, and if it seems to have been more appealing, he may decide to pursue relations with those of his own sex.

Throughout life, it is important to emphasize that experiences are drawn to us in direct accordance with the degree of intensity of the feelings we put behind our mental images. If we picture what we want strongly enough, and keep on picturing it, good or bad, we eventually get it! (I will discuss this in greater detail in Chapter 5, The Power of Imagery in Sex.)

A child exposed to any one or more of the experiences I have enumerated, desperately needs help to be able to undo the physical, mental, emotional, and spiritual harm done to him. If such help is not forthcoming from some competent, understanding source, the future for such a child is fraught with many dangers and pitfalls. His disturbed states of mind and emotions will make him susceptible for more of the same since, as I have stated, like always attracts like.

Fortunately, help is on the way for many distressed children. More and more psychiatrists and doctors are coming into an awareness of the positive and negative aspects of mind, and are developing simple, effective techniques for helping people of all ages—especially children—to remove the negative and accent the positive.

One of the most outstanding individuals in this still-pioneering type of therapy, is a remarkable man, Dr. Gerald G. Jampolsky, Director of the Center for Attitudinal Healing, Tiburon, California, whose eminent success in treating children for reading disabilities and various mental, emotional and physical difficulties, is attracting wide attention.

I know Dr. Jampolsky personally and have the deepest respect and regard for him and his advanced work, in which he makes therapeutic use of the power of visualization. Dr. Jampolsky has kindly granted me permission to quote extensively from lectures and papers he has given pertaining to the creation and application of IMAGERY as a means of enabling children to overcome physical ills and mental disturbances. While some of his imagery exercises are aimed specifically at helping the child overcome reading deficiencies, these methods can be successfully applied to all personal problems afflicting the child and are presented here in this broader sense.

When you put yourself into the children's shoes, into their parents' shoes, and then into the teachers' shoes, perhaps you can begin to get some sense of the following emotions that frequently seemed to be reinforced by each party.

The most devastating emotional factor is fear—fear that their past experiences will predict and predicate the present and future—which means more frustration, failure, fear, and guilt. From fear comes feelings of helplessness, hopelessness, futility, and guilt—then anger and hostility—sometimes direct and sometimes indirect. These children are frequently in an environment that is 80 percent doomed to fail. For them to change their imagery, to picture new attitudes toward their parents and teachers and those around their own age, and the world in general, is often so painful for all concerned as to threaten loss of self-esteem and the possibility that all efforts will go down the drain.

To eliminate and help replace the demoralizing images built into the child mind through past tragic experiences, his interest and willing cooperation must be captured by an imaginative, confidence-inspiring approach. The child needs a restoration of faith in himself and others, and an introduction, perhaps for the first time, to the power of love, expressed in feeling and personal contact.

Children in the first, second, third, and fourth grades

are not too young to be subjected to this approach. The sooner their impressionistic minds can be reached, the wrong images removed and right images implanted, the more the child will be saved from the development of antisocial, criminal and sexually abnormal tendencies.

Treating children singly and in groups, Dr. Jampolsky has them take part in mental exercises. He suggests:

Now I want you to close your eyes . . . take deep breaths . . . let them out slowly . . . inhale deeply . . . repeat several times . . . make your mind blank . . . then imagine a mental picture of yourself on a television screen. As you exhale, picture yourself letting out and getting rid of stale, tense old energy that has been connected with your bad thoughts. As you let them go, let yourself see and feel new, fresh energy flowing into you, bringing with it sensations of joy and peace and love, driving out and replacing all old feelings of fear and guilt and pains of the past!

These imagery exercises have been very effective:

Close your eyes. . . . Imagine a large container in front of you. Start filling the container with all the fears, guilt feelings, and painful experiences you can recall. Then fasten a red balloon which is filled with helium gas to the container and let go of it and see the balloon and the container disappear into the sky. Notice how much lighter and relaxed and free you feel.

Now you are going to create your own positive mental motion picture of yourself. All you have to do is close your eyes and imagine you are looking at a blank television screen. As you see it, put a motion picture of yourself on it. See yourself going through the day with a smile on your face. You are happy doing what you are doing—filled with feelings of joy, harmony, inner peace and love. See yourself not depending on anyone else. In this way you won't be disappointed or blame others for what might happen . . . or what you might or might not get. Just put your mind on doing something for others . . . and as you see yourself doing it, see others doing good things for you. Keep on seeing these kinds of pictures of yourself. Repeat them every day and you will grow to be in real life what you imagine yourself to be!

People who work with children can employ new imagery exercises like these, or can develop similar exercises to deal with individual and specific self-development needs. These exercises can bring about great and lasting changes in improved mental and emotional attitudes.

Dr. Jampolsky often uses the power of suggestion—a light form of hypnosis—to help the rebellious or defiant or bitter, defensive, uncooperative child relax and get his mind in a receptive mood so it can respond and participate in the helpful imagery exercises.

It is seldom that this form of treatment cannot be made to work. Sometimes a child is not a ready visualizer and must be reached through the medium of touch or feeling. The use of key words may help him to visualize—then he can convert words into pictures. This approach always eventually arouses feeling. Once feeling becomes associated with imagery—the pictures of what a child wants to do or be or have—feeling then leads to constructive results.

Dr. Jampolsky suggests that, whenever possible, parents as well as teachers and others who may be concerned with the child's upbringing should be brought into the act while the child is participating in the imagery exercises. He says it would be helpful if they could join in or if the parents, particularly, could be made to realize what they have been doing to themselves by their own wrong mental and emotional attitudes—and be encouraged to do something about it.

It is difficult for a child to be given a new and improved image of himself and to attempt to live up to it when he must return to a home environment that is foreign to his new way of thinking.

This new Visualizing Method is the Training Program of the future for Young People and adults. It must be adopted by all educational institutions from kindergarten through college, for the benefit of present and all future generations. In my lifetime study of mind, I have discovered what countless others are now discovering and demonstrating; that it is possible to control and direct our higher powers of mind—that they function only one way—and that the IMAGING of what you want in life is all that the God-given Creative Power needs to materialize for you in your external world, what you fear or desire. What you picture—good or bad—is entirely up to you. Right thinking and knowledge of self should begin in early childhood. It is going to take thousands of enlightened men like Dr. Jampolsky to help bring this to pass.

CHAPTER 4

The Power of Imagery in Healing

For years I have believed in the power of visualization (creating the right images of what you desire) and have had reason for doing so because this mental practice has saved my life on a number of occasions, one of them as early as the year 1920. Today, increasing numbers of the medical profession—doctors, surgeons, and psychiatrists— are adding the power of visualization to their treatments, encouraging patients with cancer and other serious illnesses to PICTURE their restoration to health in association with various medical aids.

Foremost among doctors using this visualizing method is the medical team of Dr. O. Carl Simonton and his wife Stephanie. (They can be reached through Oncology Associates, 1413 Eighth Avenue, Fort Worth, Texas.)

The two of them appeared on the program of our ESP Foundation's Sixth Annual Body, Mind and Spirit Healing Workshop, held in Dallas in 1974. They told about their

successful enlistment of the visualizing aid of patients together with medical treatments. In my opinion, this is the
most exciting and promising development in the long history of medical practice—recognition by the doctor of the
*major role the mind of a patient plays in the causation of
illness as well as its possible cure.*

There is no longer any question but that the visualizing
power of mind, rightly used, can often help bring about
a healing of physical and mental illnesses, whatever they
may be. The Simontons have given renewed hope to hundreds of so-called terminal cases who have responded to
specific methods of meditation combined with medical
treatment, a significant percentage of whom have experienced definite health improvement and longer life.

Says Dr. Simonton: "Where a patient's attitude is
positive, where he is not willing to die because he has too
many things yet to do, and where he PICTURES himself
in a restored state of health, the DIFFERENT CELLS
OF THE BODY respond to such VISUALIZATION, and
he often GETS WELL!"

When Dr. Simonton began his study of medicine, he
was shocked to learn that "the average man in our country is dead TWO YEARS after RETIREMENT!" The
statistics were overwhelming as well as frightening. When
they reached the age of retirement, many people accepted
the thought that life was about over. There was nothing of
vital interest ahead for them, and they "began withering
on the vine," to use an old phrase. It wasn't long before
their bodies, reflecting the state of mind, were "legislated
out of existence."

Dr. Simonton reasoned that if this sort of negative
picturing could have this effect upon the physical, then a
positive attitude of mind should have the exact opposite
effect. Of course, this proved easy to demonstrate. He
found that emotional stress caused by infidelity, loss of a
loved one through death, friction between friends and
relatives, feelings of helplessness and hopelessness, and
similar devastating experience, had led many people to
give up mentally and physically. If these feelings could
be removed and a positive attitude restored, it was often

possible to bring about seemingly miraculous recoveries.

Dr. Simonton also discovered that these emotional upsets usually preceded the development of cancer or some other serious affliction by from sixteen to eighteen months. Could there have been a definite connection? It appeared that way.

Delving further into the relationship between mind and body, Dr. Simonton observed that physical and spiritual depressions could result in what he called a "cancer personality." How could this develop? It became apparent that the conditions productive of a "cancer personality" had to do with self-pity, a poor self-image, a tendency to resentment, inability to forgive, failure to establish long-term, meaningful relationships, rejection by one or both parents.

Since Dr. Simonton had developed cancer himself when he was a young man of seventeen, it was easy for him to identify some of these causes as they had applied to him. When he realized what he had done to himself through wrong thinking, by freeing his mind of these emotional disturbances he was able to place images of restored health in his Consciousness. These helped lead to his recovery.

Since each patient's life had to have been associated with members of his family, the Simontons have related their healing program to the family as a unit, insisting that each family member work with the ill person. In many instances, the underlying cause of an illness may have been traceable to conflicts in the home. Until recently, the average individual has believed that cancer has been caused by outside elements of a carcinogenic nature; but now researchers and doctors are convinced that mental and emotional attitudes often have an effect upon the cells of the body, making them susceptible, in weak areas of the physical, to the development of the disease.

This realization has led doctors like the Simontons to encourage patients to combat cancer and other illnesses on two fronts: the mental as well as the physical. The resultant increase in healings has demonstrated this to be the right procedure—what is now called the Holistic Approach. Dr. Simonton says:

There are three major aspects which have to be dealt with. They are first, the Belief System of the patient; second, the Belief System of the Family; third, the Belief System of the Physician. For most effective results, these systems have to work together.

Much depends on how the patient himself responds. He is on the road to definite improvement if he can clear his mind and emotions enough to change his Belief System. Then he must be joined by the Belief of the family members. This should be nonverbal, expressed in feeling form. Thoughts can be projected. The patient will sense how relatives really feel toward him and his chances of recovery. We, as doctors, have to work with the family in the same way we work with the patient. The doctor must aid in the visualizing. He must *see* the patient getting well—see his body turning on the disease . . . beginning to fight back . . . all healing processes functioning.

The patient sometimes thinks we are lying to help him build his spirits up. He must be convinced we have absolute faith in this visualizing method of treatment. He looks to us for guidance. I have found, if I have had a bad day . . . if I let myself get down with the personal pressures that are troubling me, I have to be careful or I might communicate these feelings to patients who are in rapport with me and depending on my continuing mental support.

It should be realized that we all have cancer cells undergoing malignant changes, at times, which the chemistry of the body destroys when it is in balance. When our disturbed emotions and wrong thinking become chronic over a protracted period of time, we leave the door open for invasion of carcinogenic elements which the body no longer has the strength to resist or eliminate.

There is great healing power in LOVE. This needs to be a part of every healing treatment. If a patient feels that people don't care whether he lives or dies, it is difficult to keep his spirits high enough to aid in his recovery.

Every cancer patient is instructed to imagine, to picture white blood cells taking the cancer cells away. This simple form of visualization, practiced faithfully, day after day, has often had a definite retarding effect on the course of the cancer process.

The patients who significantly outlive their life expectancy are usually those who have the courage and faith to make use of their imagination—to create positive images—and to see these images transformed into better health each day.

Dr. Jampolsky and Cancer in Children

More and more children are today becoming victims of cancer, being faced with the prospect of death. Many parents and other loved ones, as well as doctors and surgeons, have been at a loss to know how best to cope with the child mind in such a situation.

The problem, according to Dr. Jampolsky, who is specializing in treatment of child cancer cases, is reaching the mind of the child, teaching him how to relax, and giving him a visualizing method whereby he can get over his fears and emotional turmoils of past experiences, so that he can begin to see and feel himself overcoming whatever conditions are besetting him.

We found that many of the children had poor visual memory, manifested by poor recall of dreams or by looking at an object such as a pen—and not being able to visualize the pen in their mind's eye with their eyes closed.

We therefore decided not to use the usual visualization for induction technique for children, but chose to employ kinesthetic methods, such as feeling a fur on the face, feeling a weight pull an arm down, and feeling a gas balloon lift an arm up.

This procedure turned out to be fun for them, and their easy successes at these new experiences, where they felt they were increasing their use of imagination, served only to increase their cooperativeness.

Then, as a next step, we suggested that they put themselves someplace they could enjoy being—and where they would be relaxed—such as on the beach, on a raft, in the mountains, and so on. We also guided them in rhythmic breathing.

We were aiming, of course, at eventually assisting the child in getting rid of old memories which had been painful and which were probably contributing to their present physical and mental conditions. To do this, we made an unusual visual suggestion. We told the children to put their hands on their head, to go through the skull, and gently lift out their brain, and put it on the ground in front of them. Then, we told them to take a hose in their hand and begin to wash out their brain, to get rid of all the black stuff, dirt, and grime that made up these old, painful memories. When they had done this, we told them to put their brains back in their heads, feeling that their brain was lighter, and cleaner and freer.

In this process, the children were encouraged to get rid of their old Belief Systems and establish a new Belief System that *anything was possible and nothing was impossible.* They were directed to wash away such words as "but" . . . "I'll try" . . . "it's difficult" . . . "if only" . . . "I can't"—and we pointed out that words like these tended only to create negative picture images which made the past repeat itself in the present and future.

In another visualizing exercise, we had the children see a door and imagine that their body was standing behind the door. Now they were to open the door and step into their own body . . . and once inside the body they were to picture themselves inside their blood cells . . . and to take a trip through the bloodstream through all the tissues of the body: the brain, the muscles, the skin—until they had been in every part of the house they lived in . . . and they were now to let themselves feel that they were completely ALIVE in every cell of their body and strong and healthy.

Mental Treatment of All Cancer Patients

It is the accepted judgment of the medical world that a patient who has seemingly recovered from cancer or has arrested its progress cannot consider himself to be free or rid of cancer for five years thereafter. Statistics appear to have determined this length of time before a patient can feel himself to be safe from possible recurrence.

"I question the advisability of such a powerful suggestion," says Dr. Jampolsky. "A cancer patient, in his sensitized mental and emotional condition, will live in subconscious if not conscious apprehension during those ensuing five years—and knowing, as we now do, the creative power of mind, may be contributing to a revival of the cancerous growth."

In describing his methods of treatment for all ages of patients, Dr. Jampolsky gives the following outline:

1. Both from a preventive and therapeutic standpoint, we find it helpful to give the cancer patients the option of a positive mental picture of seeing themselves improve by utilizing a variety of imagery techniques where they can imagine their cancer cells diminishing and disappearing. One does not have to wait for five years to develop this type of mental picture.

2. In some patients, we use hypnoticlike techniques to assist the patient to dissociate from his body and develop an altered state of consciousness where there is a sense of timelessness and spacelessness. We find that this method can be effective in alleviating pain. Our experience is that when one gets away from linear time concepts of past, present and future, that pain disappears.

3. We feel it is essential not only to assist the cancer patient with his mind and body, but also to assist him in pursuing his spiritual self. Optional models of viewing physical death as something real or illusionary are discussed. The utilization of altered states of consciousness and a variety of image states can be helpful to the cancer patient in what death or life means to him. It gives the patient, as well as the physician, another chance for determining what is real in this world and what is not real.

4. Our experience leads us to state that it is frequently helpful to assist the patient to revise the internal and external stress factors that can contribute to the onset of an organic disease like cancer. These stresses are quite often reviewed with the patient's eyes closed so

that visceral and muscle images can be used. Mental pictures are developed that can assist the patient in recognizing that his mind can play a crucial role in making a decision of electing to live or die.

5. Relaxation exercises that combine hypnotic and meditative techniques assist the patient to allow his mind to be relaxed and receptive. It is a way of stopping the thinking processes and getting away from logical, sequential thought action. We then find that the use of the imagination to develop mental pictures in which the patient finds himself forgiving those he has attacked or put judgment on, to be extremely helpful. This method tends to dissolve fear and lets him feel the love and oneness with his environment that was always there. It frequently permits the patient not to feel separated or fearful of death.

Summarizing his description of his advanced methods, which are not unlike those of Dr. Simonton, Dr. Jampolsky concluded: "The lay public is more and more expressing a need for a less mechanized approach to the treatment of cancer. We have attempted to create an environment where there is a more holistic approach to the patient with cancer. We have sought to let the patient take a more active role by assisting him to develop positive pictures of himself and his health processes."

From Childhood to Adulthood

In the therapy used in the treatment of children, the objective is to reach the mind of the child and help correct the wrong images and Belief Systems before they become so deeply rooted that they will be carried into adulthood and destroy whatever potential may have existed for achievement of a successful, happy, healthy life.

Millions of men and women who have not been given an understanding of themselves in childhood are trying to undo the results of their earlier wrong thinking with the help of doctors and psychiatrists—at great cost in time and money—and even then may not have been able to straighten themselves out. So often they look upon ruined lives as a tragic testimony of what might have been.

A Unique Lifesaving Use of Imagery

Norman Cousins, editor and publisher of the *Saturday Review of Literature,* was stricken in 1964, after returning from abroad, with a terrifying disease called Ankylosing Spondylitis, for which medical science said there was no known cure. The affliction was extremely painful; his body was covered with nodules and gravel-like substances under the skin, he could move his limbs only with the greatest difficulty, and at one time during his illness, his jaws were nearly locked.

Given one chance in 500 to live, Cousins knew that conventional hospital treatment, including medication, would only aggravate rather than relieve his condition. Fortunately for him, he had an understanding doctor who, conceding there was little or nothing medicine could do, decided to let his patient work out his own defense against the presumed fatal malady.

One of Cousins's first steps was to move from the hospital to a hotel room where he could be free of hospital routine and follow his own recovery program. He was like a general surveying a plan of battle. Up against fearful odds, he knew he would have to be more than a passive observer. He would have to move in on the attack. This meant organizing all his inner and external resources to stand off the inroads being made by this strange disease which was painfully disconnecting his body tissues. He could see that he would have to do something heroic to get his adrenal glands and endocrine system to working well again. If they failed, he would certainly die.

Moreover, he would have to eliminate, insofar as was possible, his exhausting emotional tensions, frustrations, fear, and rage, and fill his mind and body with massive doses of love, hope, faith and confidence, supported by a mighty will to live. Then, reminded of the often-quoted statement: "Laughter is the best medicine," Cousins hit upon the idea of providing a means of filling his mind with *laugh-provoking imagery*. To do this, he arranged for a supply of Allen Funt's hilarious "Candid Camera" films, supplemented by humorous passages from an array of funny books which were read to him by his nurse.

This abbreviated account of Norman Cousin's fight to live is not designed to be medically accurate, except to state that he combined his "laughter prescription" with tremendous doses of vitamin C—more than medical science said it was safe to take—and this highly original as well as courageous program finally won out over astronomical odds. It took him months to be completely free of all the devastation he had suffered, but today he is almost as active physically—and certainly mentally—as ever. He has long since returned to his editorial desk and his many world interests. All this is a demonstration of what Man can do if he has sufficient intestinal fortitude, vision, and the will to keep on keeping on.

The imagery-inducing laughter blotted out a variety of otherwise pain-conscious, fear-ridden images of the disease itself, which seemed bent on destroying him mentally as well as physically. Cousins's ingenious idea of occupying his mind with cheerful mental pictures was a big factor in helping restore his body chemistry to normal functioning. His cure could largely be attributable to the power of visualization.

My Own Healing Imagery Testimony

Twice during my own life, I have been faced with physical illnesses which threatened my survival—and I, like Norman Cousins, was able to save myself by employing a similar imagery technique.

My first great need to use what I called "picturization" was in 1920 when I was working for the Ford Motor Company in Detroit, Michigan. Playing tennis one day, I developed a water blister on the toe next to my big toe on my right foot. It broke open, I washed it, and thought no more about it—until the toe became infected. It grew rapidly worse. I had it lanced, but it still did not respond, and the infection developed into gangrene. The toe was badly inflamed and swollen, extremely painful.

Soon my condition reached a crisis stage, and my family physician, Dr. Garner, brought a surgeon for consultation one night. The decision was made that if I were no better in the morning, it would be necessary to take me to the hospital for a possible amputation.

When the surgeon left, I detained Dr. Garner. I told him, ever since I realized my condition was serious, I had been meditating each day, trying to picture in my mind, my toe restored to normal.

I said, "Doctor, you may not understand this. But I have the faith, the feeling, that if I could place a mental picture in my mind of my toe as it was before I developed this infection, that it would get well."

Dr. Garner looked at me skeptically. "But, doctor," I continued, "My trouble is that I am so close to my condition, every time I try to picture a healthy toe, the swollen, gangrenous image of my toe comes to mind, and I feel I am making matters worse instead of better. Now, the only way I see to get around this is to ask for help. I naturally do not want to lose part of my foot, so I am going to make what may seem like a strange request . . . "

"I'm listening," said Dr. Garner.

"Well, doctor—I feel that I am not strong enough now to overcome this condition. I need the help of a healthy mind in a healthy body. Would you, when you get home tonight, sit quietly and picture in your mind the changes you know, as a medical man, which must take place in my body and my toe—to make it heal? If you will, I'll try to picture in my way—at the same time—and we'll see what happens!"

Dr. Garner said, "Harold, if you feel it will help, I'll be glad to do it."

"Please, doctor, don't give me lip service. Don't just say this to make me feel good. You've got to *really mean it*—put *feeling* behind it—or it won't do me any good."

"How long would you like me to picture this?" asked the doctor.

"When will you be home tonight?" I questioned.

"I have one other call to make. I should be home by ten o'clock tonight."

"Can you give me half an hour?" I asked.

"You *have* half an hour," he said.

When Dr. Garner left, Mrs. Walker, my landlady, a Christian Scientist, who had been listening in, said, "Harold, would you mind if I thought along with you?"

"I'd appreciate it very much," I said. "I'm going to need all the help I can get!"

I could hardly wait for ten o'clock to come. My toe throbbed with pain. I could think of nothing else. However, at ten o'clock, I knew I had two minds working with me. Dr. Garner, several miles across the city of Detroit, and Mrs. Walker in another room in the house.

For the first twenty minutes or so, I tried to relax . . . tried to see my toe in its healthy, normal state . . . in my mind's eye. But each time I tried, the image of the gangrenous toe took possession of me. I let go of it at once and cleared my mind . . . and started over.

Then, all of a sudden, I seemed to make contact with the other minds working with me. I felt a power and a strength flash through me. And for just a fleeting second, in my mind's eye, I saw and felt my toe to be free of the affliction.

The mental relief was so great that I dropped to sleep and slept the sleep of exhaustion. The next thing I knew it was six in the morning. I awakened with a start. My first concern was to keep from moving my foot in any way that would cause pain, as it had before.

I looked down at my foot—and saw, to my amazement, that my toe's infection had broken during the night and had drained. The swelling was almost gone. I felt my body—I no longer had fever. I sat up on the side of my bed like a person coming out of a nightmare. I tested my foot on the floor—then stood up and put my weight against it. Unbelievable—there was no pain!

A great feeling of gratitude and thanksgiving came over me. At eight that morning, when Dr. Garner called, prepared to take me to the hospital, if necessary, I met him at the door in my bathrobe and slippers. We were joined by Mrs. Walker, and the three of us rejoiced at the amazing evidence of the power of visualization.

Mrs. Walker, the Christian Scientist, said she just pictured "perfection"—that the affliction had disappeared as though it had never been.

Dr. Garner said *he* had pictured what he felt, as a physician, would have to happen for the gangrenous condition to be removed.

I said, I had always felt if I could restore the pattern of a healthy toe in my mind, that it would bring about the desired result. Somehow, all three minds, working together, had produced the healing! Of course, it took some months for the gangrenous tissue to slough off, and my toe to restore healthy tissue. I still bear the evidence of this experience in a deformed toenail.

When I told a few friends of my recovery, one of them doubted my story and asked permission to write Dr. Garner about it. I have somewhere in my files a copy of the letter he wrote, which reads something like this: "It is true what Harold Sherman has told you about his recovery from this gangrenous condition. I consider it the nearest thing to a miracle that has happened in my forty years of medical practice."

There was one other time when I needed to call upon this power of picturization in an effort to save my life. We were then living in New York City. It was 1935. A man took advantage of me in a business deal and temporarily ruined me financially. We had to move from a duplex apartment on the top floor of a Central Park apartment house to the basement of the same building, and drastically change our mode of living for a time.

I knew better—but it is the closest I ever came to having murder in my heart for any person. And what did my murderous thoughts do to me? They changed my body chemistry and made me susceptible to the contraction of a fungus growth in my throat—which almost took my life.

I was shaving one morning in April 1935 when I felt a strong stinging sensation in my throat. I looked in the mirror and saw a cauliflowerlike growth which extended over the area where my tonsils had once been. I went immediately to my family physician, Dr. Seymour Wanderman, who was noted as one of the country's finest diagnosticians. He said, "Harold, I have never seen a condition like this, but it looks to me like a fungus growth, called a mycosis. Do you remember having eaten any moldy food recently?" I recalled having eaten a piece of moldy bread the day before—and Martha and I had thrown out the rest of the loaf.

Dr. Wanderman said, "Many people eat moldy food, at times, which passes through their systems and has no effect upon them. But, in *your* case, your body apparently did not resist this mold, and it has attached itself to the membranes of your throat. I hope my diagnosis is wrong. If it isn't, I must tell you that this condition could be very serious. I want to send you to Dr. Gross, bacteriologist, for a culture analysis."

When Dr. Gross read the note I had given him from Dr. Wanderman, he said, "No, no, you can't have that— it's a tropical disease!" But when he had finished examining me, he sent me back to Dr. Wanderman with a verification of his diagnosis.

While I was seeing Dr. Gross, Dr. Wanderman had been looking up reports on this mycosis in his medical books. The little-known facts were pretty grim. Dr. Wanderman and I were close personal friends. For this reason, he felt he knew me well enough not to conceal anything from me. He explained to me that this mycosis was a virulent form of fungus which fed like a parasite on the bloodstream through the membranes of the throat. He showed me photographs of patients where the fungus growth had completely closed the throat and cut off the windpipe. Only forty patients had been known to have had this affliction in this country in the past fifty years of medical history—and all forty had died within a few months' time.

It was a shock to me, of course. My mind went ahead in time. I thought naturally of Martha and our two daughters, Mary and Marcia. I was in no financial condition to leave them. But the odds, at the moment, seemed insurmountable.

"Well, Cy," I said (Cy was his nickname for Seymour), "What do you feel can be done—if anything?"

"First," said Cy, "before I try any treatment I might devise, I want to make an appointment for you with Dr. Chevalier Jackson of Temple University Hospital, Philadelphia. He is regarded as the world's greatest throat specialist. Dr. Jackson is the inventor of the bronchoscope, an instrument which permits examination of the throat and lungs. If anyone would know of an effective treatment for this mycosis, he will."

"Sounds good," I said.

Cy put in a call for Dr. Jackson and got his secretary on the line. "I'm sorry, doctor," I heard her say, "but Dr. Jackson won't be able to see Mr. Sherman. He is leaving tomorrow morning for a medical cruise around the world . . . and will not be back until the day after Labor Day." Dr. Wanderman hesitated. We both looked at each other. Then Cy said to the secretary, "Will you please put Mr. Sherman down as Dr. Jackson's first patient when he returns?"

Dr. Wanderman hung up and sat studying for a moment. "Cy," I said, finally, "from April to September is five months. What do we do from now until then—if I am still here?"

"Harold, with your permission, since there is no prescribed treatment for your condition, we're going to have to resort to things that have never been tried before. I would like to swab your throat each day with aniline dyes, with the hope that they will limit the extension of this fungus growth . . . keep it from advancing much further in your throat until Dr. Jackson comes back, has a chance to look at it, and see what *he* can do."

Cy started the aniline dyes treatment at once. They were continued until the time came for me to go to Philadelphia the day after Labor Day. In that time, the growth had slowly extended from the tonsil area, along the sides of my throat, to about a quarter of an inch from the windpipe. I was living on what amounted to a liquid diet.

Strangely enough, I was still reasonably active. There was no outward evidence of the condition except a huskiness of voice. So I would not have to combat the negative thoughts of others, I had told Martha and my mother not to speak of my affliction to anyone. My greatest trouble was my own thinking. I could picture a time when my name would be added to the statistics of those who had not survived. Then, too, I had not yet rid my mind of the hate and resentment I still felt for this man who had taken financial advantage of me.

To forgive others of any wrongs they have done you is one of life's most difficult assignments. I knew that until and unless I could free myself of all destructive thoughts, I would have even less chance of recovery.

What I needed was a powerful thought—a positive picture with which I could lift my consciousness—something that would give me hope—in which I could place my faith. I decided I would accept whatever Dr. Wanderman or Dr. Jackson would do for me, but it was clear to me that I must attract help, if possible, from some other source.

Suddenly, in a moment of prayerful meditation, an IDEA came. I heard myself saying: "Sometime, somewhere, in time to save my life, I will meet someone who knows a specific cure for the mycosis of the family Leptothrix." I began repeating this positive affirmation each night. It was the last thing I thought of upon retiring, the first thing I thought of upon awakening.

"Sometime, somewhere . . . in time to save my life . . . I will meet someone who knows a specific cure for the mycosis of the family Leptothrix."

And now the time had come for me to go to Philadelphia and meet Dr. Jackson, the country's leading throat specialist. I went with high hopes and expectations, but I was doomed to disappointment. They kept me at the hospital for ten days, wheeled me in and out of the darkened operating room at odd times of the day and night, where a parade of doctors with masks over their faces, looked into my throat through the bronchoscope . . . and I heard them say, time and time again, *"Very interesting, doctor—thank you very much!"*

I did not know until later that Dr. Jackson had wired different specialists that he had a rare mycosis case, and they had come to have a look at something they had never seen before. Cultures had been taken, of course, and I had been completely examined, but I could see nothing had been done to improve my condition.

At the end of ten days, the nurse told me to dress and prepare to return home. When I was ushered in to Dr. Jackson's office, he said, "Mr. Sherman, I have outlined a method of treatment and mailed it to your physician, Dr. Wanderman. You are to report back to him."

"But, doctor," I said. "The growth is still there. What am I to do?"

"Everything will be all right," the doctor assured me.

I took the train back to New York City and a cab directly to Dr. Wanderman's office. It was shortly after ten in the morning. "Harold, what are you doing back?" Cy asked.

"Don't you know?" I replied. "Dr. Jackson said he had written you."

"I haven't heard from him yet," said Cy.

As he spoke, the postman arrived with the day's mail. He dropped it on Dr. Wanderman's desk, and I saw Dr. Jackson's letterhead. Cy slit the envelope open, read the letter, hesitated a moment, then handed it over to me.

I was amazed at what I read. Dr. Jackson started his letter by congratulating Dr. Wanderman on his accurate diagnosis of the mycosis of the family Leptothrix. "Of course, you know, doctor," he went on, "that there is no known specific cure for this malady. We have been testing cultures in the laboratory and have found no way to control them." The last paragraph requested Dr. Wanderman to advise when the patient expired.

"Well, Cy," I said, as I handed back the letter. *"Where do we go from here?"*

"Harold," he answered, "I have been holding off doing anything drastic until I had word from Dr. Jackson, but since there is nothing he can do, I propose to fill your bloodstream more full of arsenic than the medical books say is ordinarily safe. We know that arsenic will kill both animal and vegetable life in the laboratory. Let's hope that these arsenic injections will kill off the mycosis where it is rooted in the tonsil area."

Three days a week, I was Dr. Wanderman's first patient in the morning. I took arsenic injections. Gradually, as Dr. Wanderman had hoped, the fungus growth which was caked along the sides of my throat began to recede until it had been reduced to two spots, about the size of a dime, where my tonsils had been. At this point, the mycosis resisted shrinking. Finally Dr. Wanderman told me he did not dare continue with more arsenic injections for fear of impairing different bodily organs.

"Let's hope your system has built up enough vitality to throw off what remains of the mycosis," he said. But, inside two weeks, without the arsenic injections, the mycosis began to spread again.

Throughout these months, I had kept my hopes alive by picturing each day: "Sometime, somewhere, in time to save my life—I will meet someone who knows a specific cure for the mycosis of the family Leptothrix."

One day, a friend, Sidney Esta, asked me if I would like to go with him to hear a lecture by Dr. A. E. Strath-Gordon, a British brain surgeon in World War One, who was speaking on the subject, "The Great Pyramid." The lecture was intensely interesting to me, so much so that I introduced myself to Dr. Strath-Gordon and invited him to have lunch with me the following day at the City Club of New York.

While we were eating, I had to clear my throat several times, which was so often necessary in those days. Dr. Strath-Gordon looked at me. "Are you having a little trouble with your throat, Sherman?" he asked. An *inner voice* said to me: "TELL this man!" And, for the first time, I related my experience with the fungus growth.

Dr. Strath-Gordon listened intently. When I had finished, he asked, "What is the condition of your throat now?" I told him there were just two spots over my tonsils. Dr. Strath-Gordon said, "Do you have pencil and paper?" I reached in my pocket and took out an envelope and a pencil.

"Take down this prescription," directed the doctor, and began dictating: "So many parts of creosote, so many parts of glycerine . . . so many parts of carbolic acid . . . " And so on.

"What is this, doctor?" I asked, as I took it down.

"This is a specific treatment for the mycosis of the family Leptothrix," he said.

"Where did you get it?" I asked.

"As a young doctor and surgeon, I was sent by the British government to South Africa to work with the famous Japanese scientist, Dr. Noguchi. While there, natives were dying like flies of this mycosis in epidemic form. Dr. Noguchi developed this solution. If it is used before the fungus growth has progressed too far, it cures the condition."

Like a man coming out of a long nightmare, I expressed my profound gratitude, telling Dr. Strath-Gordon of my constant prayer that I would someday meet someone like him. I took a cab immediately to Dr. Wanderman's office and told him the unusual circumstances by which I had come by this prescription.

"Looks interesting," said Cy. "Go to the drugstore and get it filled."

I returned with the solution. Dr. Wanderman soaked an applicator and swabbed my throat. There was a burning sensation. The fungus growth shriveled up . . . withdrew its roots . . . released its hold on the throat . . . dropped off—and I was HEALED!

Consider the mathematical chances against my meeting perhaps the ONE person on earth at that time who knew a specific cure for this rare mycosis! Millions to one! And yet a Higher Power in my mind arranged the circumstances by which I was led to him in time—as I had PICTURED—to save my life!

In my case, as in many cases today, I required medical as well as spiritual help. Dr. Wanderman played a vital part in keeping the mycosis under control until Dr. Strath-

Gordon could appear on the scene with the specific needed to complete the healing!

Do you wonder that I believe profoundly in the power of PICTURIZATION? That I have written about it again and again . . . that I have emphasized the one great, infallible law of mind—that "like always attracts like" . . . that what you PICTURE, good or bad, will eventually come to pass, if you keep on PICTURING it!

Right now—you may be carrying wrong pictures in *your* mind . . . thoughts and feelings which are upsetting your body chemistry . . . any chronic fear . . . or worry . . . or hate . . . or resentment . . . or irritation . . . or frustration . . . can be poisoning your system. You know this to be true. What I am repeating is not new. These God-given healing energies have always existed. We are just now discovering how to control and direct them—and the time to call upon them is when we are faced with a great personal need.

A woman wrote me recently to tell me that a friend had a tumor at the base of her brain. It was as big as an egg, and the doctors considered it inoperable. She placed her hand on it sympathetically one day . . . and said she wanted to SEE it go away. To her astonishment, the tumor disappeared under her hand! She was overjoyed and, at the same time, frightened at what had happened. Somehow, she had become an instrument for healing. What she had VISUALIZED had come to pass.

Olga Worrall, who attributes her healings to the power of God working *through* her, told me that she had helped some people remove stones from their kidneys and bladders, by saying to them, "We're going into the gravel business. I want you to mentally take a HAMMER and picture yourself POUNDING these stones into POWDER. Keep on picturing it—working at it—and I'll picture along with you that these stones will be ground and smashed to pieces!"

Says Olga, "In a few days, these people began to pass fine grains of sand and gravellike substances. X rays showed the stones were GONE!"

What do YOU want or need to happen—*to* and *for* you?

Start PICTURING it!

If you need medical help, accept what appeals to you . . . but don't stop there! Go to work on yourself— hold the right thought—the right PICTURE in your mind so that your HIGHER POWER can aid in your recovery!

(The account of these two healing experiences is contained in my book *How to Make ESP Work for You* and the one about the recovery from the gangrenous toe in *Know Your Own Mind*, but I consider these case histories so basic and so illustrative of the way this visualizing power works that I have included them in this book too.)

CHAPTER 5

The Power of Imagery in Sex

What images do you have in consciousness of your Sex Life?

Are you generally satisfied with yourself as a man or a woman?

How much has your Sexual Life meant to you?

Has it been scarred by unhappy or tragic or sordid experiences in childhood?

Or, has your introduction to Sex been uplifting, for the most part, and fulfilling?

What are your mental images of it? Tasteful or distasteful?

How much influence do you think they have been having in your attitude toward Sex today?

Would you react to sexual experiences differently now, if you had them to live over again?

Do you feel that whatever sexual experiences you are engaging in today leave much to be desired?

If so, what do you think is lacking? Has it been largely your fault or your partner's?

Whatever your sexual adventures, you carry a complete record in imagery form in your Subconscious mind of every experience, together with a memory of the feeling you had at the time.

Like it or not, you cannot escape the influence that Sex, in some form or another, has had and is having on your life. You obviously wouldn't be here but for an act of Sex. It can be assumed that you came into the world, either in or out of wedlock, wanted or unwanted, the result of the uniting of one of the millions of spermatazoa from a man with the ovum of a woman.

At the moment of conception, the design of a new human creature came into being, and the miraculous process of creation began to fashion your body, in accordance with Nature's always-original blueprint, in the laboratory of your mother's womb.

If the physical house in which your consciousness resides was not impaired by an accident of birth or a genetic deformity traceable to your parental or ancestral heritage, you have found yourself endowed with a reasonably attractive and usable body, related to a specific race and color.

The chain of creative events leading up to your appearance on earth is fantastic beyond description. If any one of your direct ancestors had died or had changed their mating selectivity on the long descending path toward your advent upon the scene, you wouldn't be here today. You are the end result of this chain and you were apparently waiting in the mysterious realm of preexistence, to be born!

The wonder of it all surpasses imagination, and yet most of us have taken life for granted, giving little if any thought to the why or how of it. We are now bringing life into existence through artificial insemination so that the identity of the father is not known—or at least kept secret or attributed to a parent incapable of conceiving.

Apparently, in whatever conditions Science devises

which provide a suitable environment in which Life can manifest itself, it is ready to appear. How and what Life fundamentally is, we do not know. We are acquainted only with the ways it comes into being and have learned in experiments with other animals how to change the design or image through cross-breeding, producing variations or improvments in certain species. However, we cannot jump from one species to another. There is an integrity in different life-forms which cannot be violated. If we try to change them, we confuse or distort the basic blueprint or image related to each species and get a distorted, deformed, lifeless result.

So—there seems to have been a creative ladder up which Life has climbed to the level of the human creature, and this evolutionary process has been protective to each species on the long journey through Time, involving millions of years. Where we have been during this, to us, timeless void, no one can say. But however infinitesimal and seemingly insignificant we may occasionally feel, we must have existed in some form from the unimagined beginning if only as an IDEA in the mind of the inconceivably great Creator. Incomprehensible causative forces down to the minutest detail must have led to a multiplication of effects which produced new causes until the time for our causative conception arrived.

Here we now are, in this moment of Time—an identity, expressing through a male or female body form—a personality in our own right—possessed of an "I am I" awareness, the product of a sexual union, and endowed with the capacity, not to create, but to pass life on in the forms of our children. We can picture the whole process— it is occurring all the time, everywhere in the universe, where Life and the potentiality for Life exists. But why we came into existence on this planet rather than any one of the uncountable number of other planets is one of the many questions we probably can never answer.

Reincarnation cannot explain it. We are undoubtedly governed by the laws of cause and effect but the Life Force, identified with us, has no need to return to another body form on the same level of existence. There is every evidence that once arriving at the level of Self-Conscious Awarness, this Life Force, as it has prepared a physical body for our existence here, has already prepared a higher vibrating spirit body for our Identity's continuing dvelopment, when we die out of this Dimension.

Our birth into the Next Dimension will be as real as our birth has been here and there will be endless opportunities to make adjustments, to correct past mistakes, to develop in character and spiritual qualities, as we progress through Time and Space, leaving countless body forms behind when no longer needed.

All this is hopefully by way of giving you a deeper appreciation of the wonder of your own existence—the real wonder of Creation—and the inexpressibly high spiritual purpose Sex was originally designed to play and which Man, gifted with free will, has chosen to shamelessly exploit, to distort, to prostitute, and defame for his own degraded uses.

Much of the true beauty of Sex has been tragically lost to mankind in these materialistic times as witness the widespread divorces, the broken homes, the runaway and wayward children, the millions living without marriage, the great numbers of babies born out of wedlock, the loss of respect for home and parents, the massive sex crimes, the countless cases of destruction of life through abortion, the popular epidemic of pornography in all mediums of communication, and the disappearance of moral and ethical codes.

Where have *you* fitted in all this? You alone can answer. I hope you have escaped most of these involvements because, if you have not, you are carrying unhappy images of past events and associations which are having a harmful, possibly degrading effect upon you to this day—and will continue so to do until and unless you can free yourself from all repressed, remorseful, and guilt feelings, and come to forgive others as well as yourself, for what they have done to you and you may have done to them.

If you are a woman who has had an abortion or given up a baby for adoption, perhaps you are wondering what might have been. Could you have managed to keep and protect this life? To give it love and care? Are you satisfied, under the economic and social conditions existing, that you did all you could have at the time? You need to know deep down inside whether what you did was right, or these feelings will continue to haunt you.

If you are a man who walked out on a trusting woman left with pregnancy or a baby because you did not want to assume your share of responsibility for an act which resulted in conception, are you plagued with disturbed images? Are you hating yourself just a little for your lack of consideration?

If you have been living with a woman or a man and have broken up, what images of this experience are you taking with you? Can you put them aside and start over with someone else, or do these images superimpose themselves upon your present thoughts and feelings and keep you from any genuine enjoyment of life?

If your marriage has gone on the rocks, and you have been blaming your mate, or think you are in love with someone else and feel you must be free regardless of what happens to the children, are you wondering if your need for a more understanding, romantic life is going to be satisfied? Or might you take some of the same mistakes into a new alliance, and if you find you have also been at fault for your marriage failure, and things don't work out, what is to become of your life?

If you, as a man or woman, have taken certain personally satisfying types of sexual practices into marriage which have been formed in childhood or in different affairs, and have expected your partner to participate in these practices with you—and find he or she does not respond for some reason—will you feel disposed to seek someone with whom to gratify these urges? Or will you try to determine what is most pleasing to your partner with the hope of helping remove a possible "imagery block" and winning his or her cooperation as a reward?

If you, as a man, are suffering from the binding influence of a "mother image," you are in great danger of being spoiled for any other woman. If your mother has been too affectionate, often innocently; if she has aroused erotic feelings in you as a baby, by too much fondling; if you have formed a satisfying sexual image of these maternal contacts, you may find that your "mother image" dominates any romantic interest you may try to have with any other woman. It can cause you to feel disloyal to the love of your mother, to feel that you are being untrue to her when you are having intercourse with your wife. These feelings can be so strong as to render you impotent. And if your mother's feelings for you, as you have matured into manhood, are equally strong, she can actually compete for your affections with your wife.

Unable to understand his mixed-up feelings, a man can feel guilty as well as frustrated. The suggestion of having intercourse with his mother is shocking, even revolting to him. He respects her too much to touch her, but he can't keep his thoughts from going back to childhood sensations when she may have bathed his genitals and played with them or kissed them, innocently unaware of any effect she might be having upon his psyche.

Many a man, held in bondage by a "mother image" complex, despairing of ever being able to free himself, has turned to other men for sexual gratification. In this way, he has never disgraced his mother; she still has her "boy," her "dutiful son," and she is happy in the thought that he has never really cared for any other woman. These sexual tragedies have occurred and are occurring with greater frequency than is often realized; they are responsible for many homosexual tendencies.

If you, as a woman, have had a father who has been too affectionate, if you have been sexually aroused by his too-ardent hugs and kisses, you may have thought yourself to be in love with him; to feel that you are "your father's girl," to feel a sense of rivalry with your mother, to fantasy yourself in bed with your father, and to resist the attentions of young or older men, whom you compare unfavorably with your "father image."

If a father is possessively proud of a daughter, he may encourage her not to fall in love by making disparaging remarks about her suitors and keeping the daughter stimulated by his own attentions.

Result; the daughter, not finding any other man that interests her, turns to members of her own sex and becomes a lesbian.

There is another way a daughter can be driven into the arms of another woman, rather than a man. A too-affectionate father's attention may be so revolting to her that a daughter resists and rejects all she can, staying away from her father as much as possible. This causes her, in time, to develop such a repugnant image of any male approach that she wants nothing sexual to do with any man—then or ever.

A realistic look at life on this planet today reveals that on what might be termed the "sordid side," the world's oldest profession is flourishing, perhaps as never before. Male and female prostitutes are operating in so-called high places and low. Millions are living openly without benefit of clergy. Religious scruples are pretty much scoffed at and disregarded. Husband- and wife-swapping is prevalent. Young people—even below the teens—are involved with sex or selling their bodies for favors.

All the media are surfeited with nudity, dramatized and illustrated forms of sex practices and exploitation of the sensual and erotic. The consciousness of people of all ages is bombarded with sex images; the philosophy of "eat, drink and be merry" is being lived to the hilt. The end and aim of life would seem to be "sex, sex, and more sex."

Not that anyone begrudges a "good time" and what it takes to have a good time. But a constant violation of an age-old adage for healthy living—"moderation in all things" is leading to uncontrolled dissipation of body and mind and loss of true human values which can only result in a mass physical, mental, and emotional sickness, eventually affecting all humanity.

We now come to one of the most flagrant and dangerous misuses of sex images which is threatening the bodies and lives of innocent men, women and children in every community, city as well as rural. It is the often-violent practice of the child molester and the rapist. Both of these lawless types are motivated by fixated sex images of sexual acts they picture themselves committing, until the urge gets so strong that they have to find an outlet for it. Then they go on the prowl, looking for victims.

The child molester as well as the rapist can appear to be decent, respectable citizens whom no one would suspect of such tendencies; they are therefore difficult to detect. But they possess what I call a "Secondary Personality" which is made up of suppressed feelings and fantasized images of sex acts which they would like to perform, given the opportunity. Every so often, the compulsion becomes so powerful that the Secondary Personality takes over and causes the individual to commit a sexual assault without fear of consequences. When the deed is accomplished, resulting in a child molestation or possible killing, or rape, the perpetrator often has an ejaculation and is immediately relieved of his inner tensions. When captured, he often excuses himself on the plea of temporary insanity by saying, "I'm not guilty—something made me do it."

It is very seldom that the sex criminal shows any remorse for his acts, or any feeling of compassion for his victims or members of their families. His Conscious Self is unrelated to the act; his Secondary Personality has retreated into the Subconscious, and this influence is held responsible so that the individual himself has no pangs of conscience. He didn't do it, and that is that. But, at times, the Secondary Personality causes the individual to review the lurid details of each attack, which again excites his sexual impulses. While the individual tries to resist, he eventually surrenders to these inner urges, blanks out, and another sex crime is committed.

To date, there is no psychological or physiological cure for a sex offender. He can be imprisoned for as long as ten years, be released on good behavior, and then commit another sexual assault. All these years he has been living on his fantasies of past child molestations, rapes, and possible killings. He has pictured himself committing these acts again and again, deriving sexual satisfaction from them, excusing his real self, as the observer, but not the activator. It is as though he is looking at mental motion pictures of another self, apart from him, performing the acts, which he is willing to let him do, on occasion, just as long as he doesn't have to take the blame.

A moral appeal, a religious conversion, a threat of punishment—even death—means little or nothing to the sex criminal. The sooner Society recognizes this fact and sees to it that such perpetrators of sexual attacks are kept confined for life, the sooner greater protection will be afforded and the more innocent children and others will be saved from possible traumatic shocks, injury, and death.

Every year there are thousands of girls, many from fine families, who run away from home, seeking fame and fortune, and are swallowed up, never to be heard from again. Some of them undoubtedly have either been captured or seduced by white slavers and put into brothels or apartments where prostitutes serve their clientele.

Some young women voluntarily enter the profession and actually defend it by claiming that they are helping relieve the sexual tensions of many men and women who can find no release elsewhere. There is a degree of truth in this as some men, who have uncontrollable sex urges, might be potential sex criminals if they were not able to visit such places every so often.

Some men and women go to brothels to satisfy a sexual craving to hurt someone or to be hurt. The first form of punishment is called *Sadism*. A man or woman derives sexual gratification from inflicting pain, physical as well as mental, on another person. These feelings have been engendered by some childhood experience, in which the individual has found it pleasurable to hurt someone else. Once this imagery has been impressed in mind, unless removed, it will stay with a person through life and demand expression from time to time, if and when any opportunity affords.

The second form of sexual punishment is known as *Masochism*. A male or female derives sexual satisfaction from the experience of being hurt, physically or mentally. It is often inspired by mental images of being humiliated or dominated. These feelings are again a carry-over from some childhood incidents when a sensual reaction has been caused by some form of punishment administered by parents or others. Simple spanking over a parent's knee has sometimes been all that was needed to give the child a sexual feeling. It has been pleasurable enough so the child was tempted to be naughty again just to invite another whipping. As adults, feeling somewhat foolish, individuals nevertheless have hired prostitutes to administer the same kind of punishment.

These mental images—stimulating the desire to hurt others or be hurt by them, and the willingness of partners to submit to or to administer such experiences—are some of the strange sexual anomalies.

Another use of Sex Imagery is masturbation which is a practice almost universally employed, at times, when people of any age feel the need of sexual relief and no safe or suitable outlet is available.

Many resort to masturbation, a word long held in disrepute, but a practice that has enabled many to avoid visits to prostitutes, while indulging in pleasant sexual fantasies as a means of simple gratification. There is nothing wrong or injurious if engaged in moderation, but many people have lived with guilt feelings because of it.

Young people, especially, would often be saved unhappy or even tragic alliances with others if they managed their urge in this way rather than in promiscuous sex adventures.

There is no final or comprehensive answer to the many problems brought about by wrong use of Sex Imagery. You can do little about the sexual state of the world. But you can do a great deal about your own experiences and attitude toward Sex. The ideal would seem to be relating your sexual desires to the feeling of Love. When sex becomes more than just a physical act—when it involves a blending of two loving images partners have for each other; when you can achieve a complete giving of yourself to the other—then something transcendent happens far beyond a mere physical excitation . . . and a loving ONENESS results!

Realizing such an experience may require releasing from mind many of your Sex Images of the past, if they may have been unpleasant or unsatisfactory. Let go of them. Clear your Consciousness. Prepare yourself for new implantations of mental pictures which can attract new and finer sexual experiences to you. This can happen with your present mate or companion; it can happen to someone who may be destined to come into your life.

Remember, if you don't change your imagery, you cannot change the things you would like to attract to you. The choice is up to you.

CHAPTER 6

The Power of Imagery in ESP

Perhaps more than most people, because of the nature of my life experience, I have been much more acquainted with IMAGERY and its overall influence on everything we think and feel and do.

As a writer, I early learned to recognize the difference in feeling between wishful thinking and imagination and the mental pictures of real events, also stored in Consciousness.

The ability to detect this difference proved of utmost importance during my experiment in long-distance telepathy between Arctic explorer Sir Hubert Wilkins and myself, when we were separated by some two to three thousand miles, in his search for the lost Russian fliers near tht North Pole.

As I, acting as receiver, sat three nights a week, from 11:30 to midnight, Eastern Standard Time, in the study of my New York apartment, I had to distinguish between the images that I felt were coming to me from the mind of Wilkins, wherever he might be in the Far North, and my imagination. I couldn't allow myself to "guess" what might be happening to him, or what had happened that day, or I would immediately bring my imagination into play.

I found that if I could make my mind receptive and let myself "wonder" what Wilkins was thinking or had been doing, a flow of images and feelings would usually come to me, which I recorded in my notebook as quickly as I could. Then I cleared my mind and started over again.

I knew that Wilkins, by prearrangement, was concentrating on me, reliving and reviewing in mental picture form, the outstanding events of the day. Each image which flashed across the inner screen of my mind carried with it a sensing of the feeling that Wilkins had had of the experience. Sometimes the feeling would be received ahead of the picture—or seem to dissolve into a picture in my consciousness.

I couldn't hold the images long. They appeared and were gone in an instant, and I had to train myself to remember what I had seen in my mind's eye, after it had vanished. How can I explain my mental sensations to you? I might liken them to a skyrocket which blazes across a night sky, leaving a luminous trail behind, which slowly dies out as you look at it. It was my job to write down as much as I could of what I had seen or was seeing, often in fragmentary form, because I couldn't catch all of it.

Once the image was gone, it could not be recalled except through memory, then only a disjointed recollection was possible, not usually in the right order. Sometimes it would require follow-up impressions to complete the picture; at other times, I would get only a part of a scene, and the rest would elude me. I learned that I couldn't strain after it or my imagination would go into action, and I would have to drop it altogether to prevent what I call "coloring."

On January 27, 1938, for example, while concentrating on Wilkins at the appointed time, the impression came to me of "a dead dog on ice," and I recorded it. Then I wondered how the dog was killed, the feeling came that it had been shot. When Wilkins's report was received from his diary, as of that date, several weeks later in New York, he had written:

> Out walking—came upon dog dead on ice—it had been shot through the head—thought about it strongly for some time—wondered reason for killing.
>
> (page 260, *Thoughts Through Space*)

In recording my impressions of the "dead dog," I had noted that I had a "strong feeling about it," and Wilkins indicated, as you have seen, that he had "thought about it strongly for some time."

Since I received accurate images so often, it led to our conclusion that feeling generated the power behind thought—the stronger Wilkins felt about something, either as he was undergoing the experience or thinking about it afterward, and trying to picture it for me, the more easily, vividly and accurately I seemed to be able to pick up the impressions.

Since these pioneering experiments, parapsychologists have repeatedly demonstrated in laboratory testing of sensitives that feeling plays a vital part in mind-to mind communication. What the Sender feels most deeply, it follows that the Receiver usually records a higher score of hits.

This has been proved in thousands of cases of psychic phenomena when mothers and fathers, husbands and wives and sweethearts have received impressions in dreams and visions of the tragic injury or death of loved ones in wars and accidents. They mentally saw these happenings or just "knew" that something was terribly wrong. In every instance, intense emotion had been involved as the endangered individual's thoughts were transmitted with great feeling to his nearest and dearest, miles and miles away.

Each night, when I had finished recording my impressions of what I felt had happened to Wilkins that day, I made typewritten copies of them and mailed them to Dr. Gardner Murphy, then head of the Psychology Department at Columbia University, who had agreed to act as observer. In this way the experiment, which lasted as it turned out for over five months, was protected by government postmark which contained its own proof that long before we could get a check report from Wilkins's diary and log of what had happened on those dates, we were already on record. When the experiments were finally concluded, and the several hundred impressions checked, it was found that approximately 70 percent had been remarkably accurate.

During the experiments, I was tormented, time and again, by my Conscious mind doubting what I had received—feeling it just couldn't be true. I never felt relieved until I received Wilkins's confirming check reports from various mailing stations in the Far North. I was not infallible, and no genuine sensitive can claim 100 percent results, despite a possible ability to get significant above-chance scores.

Should you wish to try to develop your own telepathic or extrasensory powers, it may help for me to further describe the way I see these images in my mind's eye. They often appear as you might recall from memory different scenes from a motion picture you have attended. Some of the images would probably be shadowy and indistinct, but clear enough for you to again experience the feeling at the time of the showing.

This is pretty much the way that my mind assembled and put together images which came to me from the mind of Wilkins—or images that I receive when I am trying to locate missing planes and people—and even dogs and cats and other animals!

One of the most unusual requests for psychic help came from a local Mountain View woman, Sharon Rosa, wife of druggist Van Rosa. The couple owned a large cattle ranch west of the little town on a high mountain which I had never visited. The day she phoned me, she apologized for bothering me, but said that she and her husband had operated on a badly injured cow and had left it on the top of Cow Mountain, unable to get on its feet.

When they came to care for it the next morning, they discovered to their amazement that the cow was gone! They had searched six hours for it that day, and four hours the following day, in practically every direction, up and down the mountain, through wild wooded areas, and the cow was not to be found. They couldn't imagine what had happened to it and finally decided to call me and see if I could get any impressions.

While Sharon was talking on the phone, I had put my mind on the cow and was letting my mind *wonder*. It began bringing me mental images, and I interrupted Sharon to tell her that I had seen the cow in my mind's eye—that it was in great pain and, in trying to get away from the pain had made a frenzied effort to get on its feet, and to stagger down the mountain toward a fence some hundred yards away.

"Yes, there's a fence," said Sharon, "but the cow couldn't have gotten any further—she would have been stopped by it and we could easily have seen her."

"Just a minute," I said. "I see the cow turning right and going along the fence some distance where she comes on an opening in the fence—"

"No, no—I'm sorry—there's no opening," broke in Sharon.

"Can't help it," I insisted. "I can only tell you what I mentally see. There seems to be a hole in the fence and the cow staggers through it . . . and stumbles and slides down the mountainside about a quarter of a mile, where she comes to a ravine. As she tries to climb up it, she falls, completely exhausted, and lands in the bushes. If you will go to the place where you left the cow and proceed to the fence, and follow the direction I saw the cow go, to the opening in the fence, and go on down the mountain, I feel you will find the cow."

"Well, I thank you for your help," said Sharon. "I can't believe that is what happened . . . but we'll look into it. It's the one direction we haven't looked because we were so sure the cow couldn't go far on account of the fence!"

When Sharon told her husband Van about my impressions, he expressed great doubt but agreed to drive his wife and his son Rick to Cow Mountain the next morning. He volunteered to wait on the highway below while mother and son climbed to the top of Cow Mountain, to the spot where the cow had been, Then they proceeded to follow my instructions and were astounded to come upon the hole in the fence. They went on down the mountain to the ravine—and there was the cow, now dead, lying in the bushes, exactly as I had described!

In this instance, the impressions I received were 100 percent correct. So, you ask, how did I get them? Where did they come from? I had to have gotten the information from somewhere. Did I read the mind of the cow? Of course not—but I feel, in ways we cannot comprehend, everything that happens in the universe, however seemingly small and insignificant, is somehow recorded in imagery form in a dimension I call the "mental ether."

Occasionally it is possible for a sensitive to suggest to his mind that it tune in on the vibratory existence of an experience like the "lost cow," and it will get what amounts to a pictorial playback of the happening!

Another fantastic demand was made upon such psychic sensitivity as I possessed by a woman who owned a ranch in Colorado. My Little Rock ESP Foundation office received an urgent long distance call around noon one day from a Ruth Harvey who said, "To do me any good, I must hear from Harold Sherman before sundown." As I have an unlisted number, the office relayed the call. It aroused my curiosity, and I made a point of answering immediately. You could never guess what the caller wanted me to attempt!

She reported that two teen-age girls had climbed the fence of the corral, and one of them had managed to mount one of the horses for a bareback ride. The horse took off, reared, threw her to the ground, and kicked her in the face, knocking out six teeth. She was in surgery at present, but the surgeon told them that if the teeth could be found wihin six hours, he thought he could replant them. The girlfriend who had accompanied the injured young lady was also in the hospital, in a state of shock, and could not remember the details of the accident or the approximate place they had been in the pasture when the teeth were lost.

The Question: could I re-create the scene with my ESP and pinpoint the place in the pasture for them to look for the missing teeth? The request seemed so ridiculous and farfetched that I almost begged off attempting to be of help. However, I was amused to think that anyone would place such faith in a psychic. Perhaps it would be worth a try. The worst that could happen would be a miss.

As Ruth Harvey was conveying this information, I fixed my mind on the situation and images began to form. I stopped her and announced that I was getting impressions.

"I am mentally standing, facing the front of your ranch house," I told her. "To the right of it and about a quarter of a mile behind it, I see two buildings. One seems to be a red barn, in the corner of a corral."

"That's right," she confirmed.

"My mind goes beyond these buildings and follows along the fence line several hundred yards. Now I see the two girls climbing the fence. They get over into the pasture and approach three horses."

"Yes, we have three horses," said Ruth, at her end of the phone.

"The girls try to catch one of the horses, but he shies away. Then they manage to get another of the horses over against the fence, and one of the girls climbs the fence and slides onto the horse's back. The moment she does, I see the horse whirl around and run straight out from the fence, which is about two hundred yards from the corner of the corral. He dashes about a hundred yards out into the pasture, jumping and kicking, and throws the girl off, one of his hoofs striking her in the face. It's a big pasture, but that is as near as I can come to telling you where you might look for the teeth."

"Thank you, Mr. Sherman," said Ruth. "This gives us a specific area to start looking. We'll go right out while there is still sunlight—and begin searching!"

It was several days before I got a report. Then I received a letter from Ruth Harvey with the astounding news. *They had found one of the teeth* in the tall grass of the pasture right where I said they might be. They were still searching for the others when word came from the surgeon, who had taken some one hundred and sixty stitches in the girl's face. She was so badly injured that he couldn't replant the teeth, so it was no use looking further.

Ruth said that the girl's parents, who had not wanted her to call a psychic for help, now were so impressed that they wanted to read and know all about ESP.

Ingo Swann, an artist whose spectacular concepts of the cosmos have been captured on canvas, is also one of the most remarkable sensitives I have ever known. When we met in New York where he lives and where I used to live quite some years ago, we had an instant meeting of the minds. It led eventually to my being invited by Ingo to participate with him in a series of psychic probes of the planets Jupiter, Mercury and Mars.

Scientists Hal Puthoff and Russell Targ, at Stanford Research Institute, agreed to monitor the experiments. At appointed times, Ingo, either in the laboratory at Menlo Park, California, or in his study in New York, and I, in my home near Mountain View, Arkansas, simultaneously projected our minds into space and recorded impressions of what we psychically saw or sensed there.

The results obtained astounded us and also astounded some scientists and astronomers, because Ingo and I, functioning independently and without any prior discussion of these probes between us, reported pretty much the same psychic sensing of conditions in and about the respective planets.

Recognition of our work was included in a comprehensive article titled: "What Do We Really Know About Psychic Phenomena?" which appeared in the August 1977 issue of *Reader's Digest*. After reporting various researches and achievements of psychically gifted men and women around the world, sociologist author Laile E. Bartlett had this to say:

> But these are minor accomplishments compared to what Swann and his colleagues seem able to do on their own. Once, filled with ennui by months of lab work in California, Swann phoned his friend, psychic Harold Sherman, 1,500 miles away in Arkansas, and proposed they take a 600-million mile trip together: "go" simultaneously to Jupiter, which neither of them knew anything about, but by which Pioneer 10 was scheduled to pass. Sherman agreed. Their respective observations of colors, landscapes, atmosphere and other conditions were filed the next day with astrophysicists and showed remarkable convergence. Nor were they far off from Pioneer 10 data.
>
> Challenged by a science editor, they turned their attention to Mercury, by which Mariner 10 was soon to pass and radio back data. Prevailing opinion was that Mercury had neither atmosphere nor magnetic field. Yet each psychic reported a thin atmosphere and a magnetic field—confirmed by Mariner 10 within the month.

At this writing, Ingo's and my psychic probe of the planet Mars, has not been evaluated to the point that a report can be made on it but the indications are that the results will prove to have been even more significant.

I have been asked to explain as best I can how I prepare my mind for such an experiment. I cannot speak for Ingo and the procedure he uses, but my method is simply to make myself temporarily unself-conscious of my physical surroundings, to fix my conscious mind's attention on the target or objective, at whatever seeming distance, and let himself "wonder" what exists at that point. Apparently some inner faculty of mind makes instant contact, unlimited by Time or Space, with the area it is directed to concentrate upon. If it were possible to hold the mind's attention on the locale or person, once contact is made, for more than the split second of initial contact, then I have found that a state of awareness can be retained long enough to bring back reliable data on what may exist at that point in imagery and feeling form.

In tests given him at Stanford Research Institute, Ingo Swann has demonstrated, time and again, the ability of what is called "remote viewing." He has been able to "see" what is occurring at a distance and the nature of the surroundings, even drawing corroborative pictures of places where scientists have gone, on sealed instructions, to test his psychic observational capacity.

The functioning of mind often combines clairvoyance with telepathy in achieving its "remote viewing" results. (Clairvoyance is the ability to sense and to see conditions existing at a distance.) In any and all cases, a form of mental imagery is involved.

Perhaps if I quote from a portion of my recorded impressions of the planet Jupiter, it will give one more of an understanding of just what form this feedback of planetary images took.

. . . Now I am suddenly projected to a point where I feel I can see Jupiter itself—a spectacle beyond description. It looks like it is bulged in the middle of its gigantic ball-like shape. It is a gaseous mass of myriad colors— yellow, red, ultraviolet, some greens—like a great fireworks display. There must be many chemicals and elements involved beyond my understanding.

A large red mass is moving across the face of Jupiter, from right to left, followed by a darker cloud of immense size. It is an elongation which stretches for miles and miles—a swirling mass as though generated and added to by eruptive magnetic and gaseous forces coming from the interior of Jupiter, which seems more liquid or vaporous than solid. Strange, I can see ice crystals—they are shimmering, like trillions of silver needles—and I am wondering if they are not icy cold? They seem to be nearer the surface, at different levels.

I wish I could see through the enormous cloud cover which must be miles deep. It billows and leaps, with a changing yellow and red and green incandescence, as though reflecting great magnetic fires from some far-down source.

Now I suddenly seem to see through and catch sight

of a reddish-brown formation extending in a curved line as far as my mind's eye can see. Can it be Jupiter's earth crust? It looks almost metallic—molten in spots—red-hot—great vapors seething through . . . it gives me a dizzy feeling to look at it.

I wonder if Ingo is getting anything like this . . . (he was!)

I don't know how close Pioneer 10 is destined to come to Jupiter on its pass-by, but it looks like it will eventually encounter powerful magnetic forces, winds of terrific velocity, and gaseous masses of possibly poisonous and damaging nature. The atmosphere seems unusually dense on some levels and extremely rarefied in others. There appear to be high volcanic peaks—great cones rising some miles in the air, and deep, frozen-looking, crystal-covered valleys. There must be water—probably mostly solidified or in vaporized form.

I don't get any sensation of heat or cold . . . and I don't hear what I see. It's like a gigantic silent movie . . . but I feel what I am seeing and perceiving deeply—and it is awesome . . .

. . . I suddenly feel tired . . . somewhat sapped of energy . . . I am conscious of my body . . . I have to collect my senses. I have a strong heady sensation . . . congested . . . like waking up from a sleep with faraway feelings . . .

I now hear Martha calling me from the house. I am in my special concentration room in our annex building out back. She says Stanford Research Institute is on the phone, wanting to get a recording of my Jupiter report so they can compare it with Ingo's just-completed probe.

This was pretty much the way these psychic probes were conducted—and the way they went. I was glad and honored to have been a participant because this was the first time since my pioneering experiments in long-distance telepathy with Sir Hubert Wilkins in 1937–38, that I had been given opportunity to test such "remote viewing" under scientific observation. From two to three thousand miles to some 600 million was quite a mental leap!

CHAPTER 7

The Power of Imagery in Mass Consciousness

Many scientists still express doubt that the mind is able, on occasion, to go ahead in time and sense or foresee events that are getting ready to happen.

Years ago, I discovered during my long-distance telepathic experiments with Sir Hubert Wilkins, that my mind, at times, brought me images of experiences that had not yet occurred. For example, Wilkins was as surprised as I was to observe that I had recorded a prediction that something was going to go wrong in the crankcase of his plane six days before it actually happened. How the mind could sense such a thing when neither Wilkins nor any members of his crew knew of the approaching mechanical difficulty in advance, was utterly baffling.

Of course, there had to be a logical explanation—and after a number of accurate precognitions had been repeated several times, I finally hit upon a theory which I believe stands up today.

The universe is ruled, as I have said, by the laws of Cause and Effect. Since there is a cause behind everything which eventually materializes into a real-life experience, a sensitive seeking knowledge of the future, need only tune in on the causative forces existing at the moment, and progress them ahead in time like a computer until they arrive at the effect, which reveals itself in the form of a series of mental images.

It doesn't seem to make any difference if the causes are animate or inanimate, or both. The mind somehow puts them all together and comes out with a potential end result, taking every possible relating cause into account. As the causative forces change, the effect automatically changes, and a so-called seer can be right in a prognostication when originally made—but a subsequent change in the causes can alter the effect, and what was first predicted will not happen.

My friend Ingo Swann shared my concern about world conditions. It led him to wonder, in May 1973, if a small group of selected psychics who had established a "track record" in making accurate predictions of coming world events, might test their precognitive abilities by setting their minds on the future, under observed conditions, and see if there might be a significant degree of agreement in their impressions.

He broached the subject to Willis Harman, director of the Educational Policy Research Center at Stanford Research Institute, who offered to monitor such an experiment and to specify guidelines for the psychics to follow. He proposed that the psychics chosen, who turned out to be James Neyland, Ingo Swann and myself, center their minds on the social and economic and other national and world trends in five-year segments: 1973 to 1975, 1975 to 1980, 1980 to 1985, and so on, up to the year 2000.

A full composite report of the results achieved is contained in Ingo Swann's remarkable book *To Kiss Earth Goodbye,* which was finished in July 1973, before the short Mideast conflict broke out and the Arabs cut off the oil supply, which was predicted in advance in my own recorded impressions. Each of the three sensitives independently pictured similar happenings, a not very cheering outlook for the world in general, until the turn of the century, unless some radical new program could be instituted by governments to lessen the threat of another war and other forms of destruction.

In his book, published in 1975, Ingo Swann, in commenting on the premonitory experiments, wrote:

> There was no direct evidence in July 1973 that the events portrayed were likely. In the interim, enough time and events have passed to show a high correlation for the pre–1975 predictions, with actual trends as they have come to pass, enough correlation at any rate to indicate that prophetic abilities were present in all three subjects and that the prophetic abilities aligned with each other to an amazing degree.

Here is a condensed summary of the images of the future which came to me as I concentrated my mind on the assignment. James Neyland and Ingo Swann were directing their thoughts in their way and were recording much the same overall impressions.

Today, world mass consciousness is in a state of upheaval—the people in the so-called "have not" nations are commencing to assert themselves, usually in violent form. . . . The people will vent their anger on capitalistic countries, especially the United States.

The Mideast is a dynamite key. Savage hatred between Arabs, Egyptians, and Jews will defy all peace efforts and explode in unparalleled acts of sabotage—if not a quick, devastating war—which, unless checked by powerful intervention, will seriously involve the United States and Russia.

Most threatening of all to world peace and survival may well be the cutting off of oil, the wanton destruction of refineries, regardless of the cost to the countries themselves. . . . It seems to be in the potential of the intense feelings which are building up and can materialize into destructive action. The United States will be bitterly assailed for siding with Israel. The same conditions will prevail between the Catholics and Protestants in Ireland.

As I look realistically into the future, I see, unhappily, tragic events growing out of wrong thinking and wrong conduct in so many areas of life in the United States, and in the world for that matter, that will permit little basic happiness or security in the years ahead.

Selfishness, greed, and shortsightedness have brought on a pollution crisis which is already beyond the point of control and will become so threatening to the health of great masses of people that industrial operations as well as agricultural production will be seriously affected, repercussing upon our economy, with the environmentalists and the ecologists at war with the economists and the high-pressured politicians and government leaders.

The practice of imposing the cost of all changes on to the consumer will reach the saturation point and bring about increasing protests and boycotts, with the price spiral going on up despite all attempts to bring things back into some semblance of balance. The Nixon administration, reeling under the ever-widening Watergate scandal, will continue to lose the confidence and respect of the U.S. citizens who will not know where to turn for new leadership, either in or out of government. . . .

If public confidence becomes too badly shaken and we are headed for a recession, which is definitely a possibility, a type of martial law may occur leading to a new form of government. The next few years now loom as threatening to our very way of life, particularly if the American dollar and our monetary troubles cannot be stabilized. Money values will drastically change which will have an impact on welfare, social security and other programs, as well as wages.

The minority groups in the United States such as the blacks, the Indians, the Puerto Ricans, the Mexicans and others, have not given up their struggle for greater economic consideration and more equalized treatment. As their financial and social plight is not alleviated and their living conditions improved, the racial elements among them can be expected to break out in greater acts of violence and sabotage than heretofore, in which some white-collar workers, hardly less neglected, will join.

We are moving, on this planet, into a synchronization

of crises of such a multiple nature as to paralyze the thinking and administration of world leaders. All of these crises, with hardly any exception, will have been the result of man's wrong thinking—his self-seeking, materialistic attitudes, his lack of vision. Now, having done too little and too late, having tried to postpone or disregard steps which should have been taken in many areas of human need, mankind will be confronted with the tragic effects of causes set up in years past and which are reaching a devastating harvest.

Most critical of all for humanity, is the coming ENERGY CRISIS. Unless a new form of energy is developed to replace oil and gas; unless new convertible uses of crude oil can be invented; unless a greater conductivity can be given to metals so that electrical and magnetic forces can be taken directly from the air or the universe, the fight for possession of the present existing fuel supply will bring about the most frightful war in all history.

The NEED is so urgent that it is going to be a race with time as to whether or not this ENERGY problem can be solved and save the world from a holocaust. Apparently, even if new sources of energy could be discovered or developed, it would require two to three years and more to become operative . . . and time is so crucial that it may not give opportunity to avoid this horrific potential.

As if what Man has been doing to himself and his natural resources is not enough, Nature is getting ready to rebel against the rape of her bounteous possessions. It no longer requires a seer to predict what seismologists now feel may happen any day—major earthquakes in the Los Angeles and San Francisco areas; in Alaska, even along the East Coast and in the New York City area, South American countries, Japan, Turkey and other places. Hardly any part of the earth seems immune today. This is true also of the threat of tornadoes, cyclones, hurricanes, floods, and other climatic disasters of unparalleled character.

Atomic tests and the colossal pollution have upset the magnetic currents surrounding and within the earth so the planet itself is wobbling on its axis. This sounds like the prophecy of doom, but it is clear to me that unless world leaders recognize the potential they have created and are creating for self-destruction, and work out an emergency program of a strict and cooperative nature, we are headed for economic, social, and material chaos.

Despite increased billions poured into its attempted correction, including the cost to business and industry of such problems, the alcoholic and drug situation, is destined to worsen because the millions of men and women and young people affected have to be reached individually and straightened out mentally, emotionally, and spiritually. There are not sufficient medical and psychiatric facilities to make such individual treatments possible. The liquor monopoly is doing nothing to help solve this problem while publicly lamenting those who drink too much; and the suppliers of marijuana, heroin, LSD, and the like, are so politically and commercially involved that the traffic cannot be adequately controlled.

The United States is in the relentless grip of a war economy, and war or the threat of it in some form will continue in the pretense that it is necessary for national defense. Every kind of deception will be employed, as now, to gain support for the Pentagon military operations until Congress belatedly, under pressure of the voters, asserts or tries to assert its representative power. This will lead to the severest kind of conflict between the president, as commander-in-chief and the civilian arm of government, with the realization that the people no longer have control of their government; that the power has been usurped by the president and his military advisers and can lead to new involvements beyond Vietnam.

The monumental degradation of thousands of our young men in Army, Navy and Air Force, many of whom are returning home maimed in body and spirit, victims of drugs, liquor, sexual imbalance, will be realized more and more as these people return to civilian life mentally and emotionally disturbed, unable to adjust to their home environments, still imbued with the trained killer instinct and driven by feelings of frustration and resentment. They can and will take an active part in any major riots or protests against a possible recession and other national disorders.

As a concatenation of all the previously mentioned forces, citizen morale will be seriously affected; attempts to curb INFLATION and reduce POLLUTION will not keep prices from rising but will lead to increased unemployment, industrial shutdowns, foodstuffs in short supply, and massive discontent and concern. If martial law is not invoked, communities will be without Law and Order and there may not be sufficient armed force or police authority to protect innocent citizenry even so.

A not pretty PICTURE presented to a mind that attempts to look realistically into the FUTURE. To think that this earth, ravaged as it has been, still possesses such bounteous resources, rightly protected and used, is headed for man-made disaster and can, in our time, within the date of 1990, be on the way to another DARK AGE!

With this as a beginning, based on present existing causes, my impressions were extended in segments of five years, until the end of the century. They expressed optimism with the creation and installation of new ways and facilities of living IF Man moved in time to correct major threats to his continued existence. However, these more assuring predictions were tempered with the realization that Man, through his bloody past, has changed only by virtue of the compulsion of disastrous circumstances he has brought on himself, and he will change only today when he has sufficiently punished himself by self-created disasters and knows that he must do something drastic, at all costs, in an attempt to save himself and his world.

It is my feeling that there is a vibrational interrelation between all elements in the universe, and when any of them get out of balance, they affect every other element with which they are in contact. Thus Nature reflects man and man reflects Nature.

Psychokinesis has proved that Mind can influence Matter, indicating that the Intelligence in all life is the animating force and can and does exercise control in various degrees over the particles and molecules (for want of proper words to describe) in animal bodies as well as in particles (objects) outside the body.

Apparently the higher the degree of Intelligence, the higher the degree of control. Since Man seems to be the most intelligent creature on earth, his dominion over the elements about him should be the greater, as well as his capacity to create his world from the different elements and forms of life.

When you magnify Man's individual consciousness by Mass Humanity, it should be understandable that the "vibratory effect" of mass thoughts and feelings must have a profound influence upon the planet itself as well as all peoples and all life on earth.

This adds up to effects upon Man's environment:the pollution of air, land, and water; every phase of society and civilization, the economic, social, political stresses and strains; the disturbances in geological structures, and the trend and nature of Man's thought.

My predictions have been based largely on my sensing of the mood and nature of MASS CONSCIOUSNESS in various areas and the impact it is having both as applied to the present and the future. Because of the difference in MASS THOUGHT, different countries or nations will reflect different conditions which will only change as thought changes.

It is important to remember that whatever seems destined to happen MUST have grown out of the CAUSATIVE FORCES existing at the moment. Since "like always attracts like" in the realm of mind, each CAUSE will always create an EFFECT after its kind. Only the subsequent superimposition of a STRONGER CAUSE can change the EFFECT and the nature of the eventual happening.

WHY HAVE I PAINTED THIS GRIM PICTURE OF THE POSSIBLE CONSEQUENCES OF MAN'S WRONG THINKING? ONLY BECAUSE IT IS SO VITALLY NECESSARY FOR HUMAN BEINGS TO CHANGE THEIR ATTITUDE TOWARD THEIR FELLOW MAN AND THEMSELVES, BEFORE IT IS TOO LATE. I HAVE ONLY REPORTED WHAT I HAVE SEEN, LOOKING AHEAD IN TIME . . . WHAT NEYLAND AND SWANN HAVE ALSO

SEEN . . . WHAT SCIENTISTS, STUDYING ECO-
NOMIC AND SOCIAL TRENDS ARE NOW SEEING
AND CONFIRMING . . . THIS MAY BE MAN'S
LAST CHANGE TO KEEP EARTH'S BLOODY HIS-
TORY FROM REPEATING ITSELF!

CHAPTER 8

The Power of Imagery in Dreams

What are dreams?

Of what substance are they composed?

What influence do dream images have on people?

How many dreams are caused by physical disturbances like indigestion, fears, worries, repressions?

What effect do alcohol and dope have on dreaming?

What makes some dreams garbled and distorted?

Can symbolic dreams be correctly interpreted?

Can a sleeping person pick up telepathic images from an individual who is awake?

Is it possible to see dream images of the future?

Are some dreams made up of memory images of past experiences?

Can the nature of dreams reveal the character and sometimes the motives of an individual?

Can a creative mind stimulate the imagination, during sleep, to produce images of new ideas and inventions?

Can dreams remove a mental block and reenact a forgotten past?

These questions and many more pour in as you give thought to the mystery of sleep—and what happens to the human psyche during sleep.

Everyone dreams at one time or another, and scientists say we dream every night, or whenever we drop to sleep, whether we have any recollection when we awaken or not. The source of most dreams comes from our memory storehouse which contains a continuous record, in imagery form, of everything that has happened to us since the moment we were born. The "videotape" recording of our mind never stops running. It keeps on functioning during sleep, giving us a subconscious awareness of everything within reach of our five physical senses, as well as our extrasensory faculties.

In a remarkable book, *Dream Telepathy,* Drs. Montague Ullman, psychiatrist and psychoanalyst, and Stanley Krippner, psychologist, heads of the dream research team at Maimonides Medical Center's Dream Laboratory in New York City, present the evidence of a ten-year study, proving that "thought images" can be transmitted by one individual to another who is in the sleep state, causing the sleeper to dream of the image—usually a photograph of some scene or a work of art.

Selected subjects—men and women—were put to bed in a laboratory room, their physical reactions monitored by instrumentation, while in another room an agent concentrated on pictures chosen to have emotional appeal so the transmitter could engender a feeling of his own to add intensity to his visualization.

It was found that if the sleeping subject knew and had a feeling for the transmitting individual, this subconscious rapport seemed to make possible more accurate dream impressions. Even so, it was also determined that strangers, if they could visualize with sufficient intensity, could "get through" to the mind of the sleeping subject.

It was the theory of Drs. Ullman and Krippner that telepathic transmission of thought images could be more easily performed when the resistance of the Conscious mind was removed through sleep. This seemed to have been conclusively demonstrated during their ten-year experimentation.

Both doctors stated:

> We firmly believe that an important ingredient in the success of experiments in dream telepathy over waking telepathy, established by quantitative testing, is the use of potent, vivid, emotionally impressive human interest pictures to which both agent and subject can relate.
>
> . . . People tend to dream about themselves and other people. It is relatively rare for anyone to dream about an unpopulated scene or a thing unconnected with a specific person. The targets which are incorporated most easily into dreams generally depict people and are often emotional in character, which is why we have relied so heavily on art prints rather than magazine pictures. If there is a person in the target picture with whom the dreamer can identify, a telepathic incorporation is more apt to occur. If the dreamer is a male, he tends to have more dreams about sex and aggression than a female.
>
> . . . We have seldom had a "miss" when the target shows someone eating or drinking. Religion is another theme that comes through strongly in the telepathic dreams of both sexes.

In my opinion, these Dream Telepathy tests have made a significant contribution to the knowledge of the functioning of mind in the sleep state. They have demonstrated, for one thing, that all dreams are not caused by indigestion or your fears or worries, but that a sizable percentage may have an outside origin.

Since we now know that our minds are actually transmitting and receiving instruments, then it becomes understandable that the feeling-charged images from friends or loved ones often reach us, awake or asleep, whether we are conscious of it or not, and leave their impressions upon us.

Visualize the vast number of frequencies carrying radio and TV programs through the air, of which we are not aware until the proper receiving instruments have converted them into sound and sight.

In much the same way, what I call the "mental ether" is filled with untold numbers of thought images from the minds of all human creatures on earth. We exist in an ocean of thought vibrations, protected by what might be described as a "magnetic insulatory shield" which permits our mind to function, ordinarily, without interference or invasion.

There are times, however, in the sleep state, when a strongly impelled, emotionally charged thought image breaks through this shield of protection and implants itself in our consciousness and gives us an awareness of something that has happened or is happening, usually to a friend or loved one.

An outstanding illustration of such a dream experience has been related to me in a letter from Mrs. H. G. of New York, who writes:

> I am fortunately blessed with unusually sound, easily-come-by sleep, and had retired at my usual hour of about 10:30 P.M. (11–18–70) when I suddenly found myself wide-awake. I remember saying to myself, "This is ridiculous. Why am I so wide-awake?" I was unable to go to sleep, rose and started to read Fosdick's *The Meaning of Prayer*. The clock said 1:00 A.M. It suddenly came over me very strongly that something had happened to my very dear friend Patricia. I could no longer read, but paced until 3:00 A.M. before I finally got to bed again. By 7:00 A.M. I was on the phone speaking to Patricia. About 12:30 A.M., while her husband was paying the cab driver, and his back was turned, she had been badly mugged and robbed in the hallway of her building. I did not go to work that day but hurried over to care for her and her youngest child, my godson. We both felt that this was clearly extrasensory perception, since the feeling and the timing when she needed me were quite accurate.

The files of our ESP Foundation are filled with evidential case histories like this. Mrs. H. G. was shocked into wakefulness when the first "thought waves" struck her consciousness. It took her some minutes before she could determine what had happened and to whom. Finally, her subconscious mind released the rest of the information it had received—that something tragic had happened to her friend Patricia. It was only then that she was able to do something about her dream experience.

Sleep is often called "the little sister of Death" because when you temporarily lose consciousness, you are not aware of your identity. What becomes of your identity, that something which says "I am I" to you, is an unsolved mystery. Does it still remain in your body or does it go some place, at times, and return from somewhere on awakening?

As a possible explanation, it is worth speculating that we may all possess what might be described as a "higher vibrating spirit form" in which our Real Self resides, and that often, during sleep, we leave the physical and enter the Next Dimension, where we are to exist when earth life is over.

Occasionally, on awakening, we carry over dreamlike recollections of people we have seen and places we have been. They could be friends and loved ones who have gone on—or persons and faces who appear to be new to us, but are no less real. How did the mind conjure them up and present them on the stage of our dreams?

If contact has actually been made by a spirit entity, and we cannot be sure, of course, it may have been for the purpose of conveying a personal message. Such attempted tranmission is usually in the form of a vision or dream sequence. It is seldom, however, that the impressions can get through to our point of conscious awareness in a clear, unadulterated form. The interference of your imagination can easily become activated and build upon or distort the images which are entering what I call your "mind circuits."

When you have the experience of a dream which you know is "more than a dream," it is wise to have a note pad by your bed so you can record all you can remember while the scenes and feelings are still fresh in mind. I dream a great deal and many dreams do not make sense, but each time an unusually vivid and realistic dream occurs, I try to remain in the twilight zone of sleep as I awaken my wife Martha and ask her to write down what I am about to dictate.

If Martha is not available, I get out of bed, grab notebook and pen, and, without forcing, in a half-dreamlike state, I try to relive what I just experienced, calling it forth from my memory. Sometimes I have to record the ending of the dream before my mind can go back to the start, and piece it all together. I have learned to recognize the difference in feeling when my imagination tries to help me out and add some details which do not belong.

If the dream is not related to a possible spirit message but has to do with the solution of a personal problem, or an event that appears to be coming toward me in time, I exercise the same care in trying to prevent any possible "wishful thinking" or fear or worry, from intruding and garbling or falsifying the impression.

With a little practice, you can learn to keep your imagination out of the way and your attention centered on the dream impressions that are coming to you, either from Higher Sources or from your own creative powers.

You may have heard the expression "dreaming true." This means the developed ability of an individual to get answers to his personal problems through his dreams. The method is simple but often very effective. If you have a problem which seems to defy solution, take a few meditative moments before retiring. Review in imagery form the situation that has brought about the problem. In so doing, you will be giving to the Creative Power within all the ingredients you know that have contributed to the problem. Since you have not consciously been able to find an answer, now prayerfully direct your Creative Power to work out the solution while you sleep. Then do everything possible to put aside your fears and worries and apprehensions so they will not paint the wrong pictures of what you do not want to happen.

Be prepared to have your mind give you a dream enactment of what you should do to solve your problem, or to awaken in the morning with a vision or an idea that has been worked out on Subconscious levels during the night.

Many dreams are obviously caused by indigestion or other physical disturbances such as tensions due to fears and worries. These can bring on nightmares with scenes of violence played out upon the motion-picture theater of your mind, so seemingly real as to make you cry out in terror during sleep, or awaken shocked and frightened. This is particularly true when repressed sexual urges dramatize themselves in the form of dreams wherein a person may find himself participating in sex acts he would not perform in real life—or is made the victim of such acts.

Excessive drinking can produce *delirium tremens* which, in addition to trembling, sweating and anxiety, bring on hallucinatory dreams and visions. The wild imagery resulting provokes great fear and revulsion. The images of past unhappy experiences are all jumbled together in a paroxysm of feeling, often fantastic, extremely gruesome, and threatening.

Other types of dreams and visions are created by use of various drugs and narcotics such as marijuana, cocaine, heroin, LSD, peyote, and others. These often produce imagery of a most inviting sensual nature, pleasing to the user but often destructively habit-forming. They create illusions of grandeur, of great power, of other-dimensional existences, of erotic sexual potencies, and a disinclination to participate in earthly life or the assumption of any personal responsibility. These are the hazardous dream worlds into which too many participants are today being led in an attempt to escape from a possibly too-painful reality.

Men and women who possess extrasensory abilities often experience unusually accurate and meaningful dreams. This representative case was reported to me recently. It is from a Mrs. C. Z. of Wyoming and I am reproducing it exactly as written to me:

Dear Mr. Sherman:

I am thirty-three, married, and have one child. I have been experiencing dreams which I can't explain. They are so real, it feels as if I am really there. I have had this since my twenties, never thought too much about it till last summer. My nephew went to Italy for three weeks.

One night, while asleep, I heard him talking, woke up with the feeling (I guess I was just dreaming). Three weeks went by and we picked our nephew up at the airport, and while we were on our way home, he was talking about his trip. I stopped him and said, "Let me tell you. I recall in my dreams one night seeing a cave on water. The water was very rough. We got off a large boat onto a small rowboat. We came to a cave on water and had to bend down to go through the opening. It was that small. (I described the opening.) Inside a person was selling items."

When I told my nephew, he said, "That's exactly right, except the person was selling them on the outside." He said the water was rough and they were debating if they would go on the small boats.

I have had other experiences the past winter. While asleep, I saw a jeep and I sensed a man was hurt. I felt not bad, then saw another fellow help him. I woke saying to myself, "I wonder if I saw an accident," since it had been snowing that night. That morning, my husband went out to our garage to remove the plow off our jeep after he had plowed our driveway. The pin which holds the plow on was frozen, and he tried several times to loosen it. All of a sudden it flew back with great pressure and hit him in his left eye. He walked away from the jeep and my son helped him. Did I see this before it happened? By the way, his eye is fine now.

Let me say here that often, when one dreams of a friend or loved one who has been injured or in some tragic situation, even death, the tendency of the mind in a dream is to protect from a shock reaction. In this case, Mrs. C. Z. saw a man hurt and helped by another man, but the two were not identified as her husband and son. All the other particulars were correct.

Mrs. C. Z. continues with her report:

I have had still other experiences but there is one thing that happened to me I would love to have explained.

About four months ago, while asleep, I woke quite suddenly and saw a young man with a lot of hair, who was very tall. I felt no fear and, in fact, never thought about trying to move, except I did move my eyes, opened and closed, very wide. After what seemed a short time, his image faded, just like I had always seen in movies about ghosts. At that time, I knew I was not asleep! I woke my husband about it minutes afterward, and only then became frightened because I didn't understand what it meant. I haven't told anyone about this except my husband and family. Can you tell me what happened?

This is an outstanding instance—one among many that are being reported—which gives evidence that some part of a person's consciousness either leaves the body or enters what is called "the astral plane," where contact is made with possible "spirit entities" or "thought forms," and when the sleeper is awakened too suddenly, is still able to psychically see scenes and figures existent in this Higher Dimension.

We raised the question in the start of this chapter: Of what substance are dreams composed?

They take place in the Mystery Theater of the mind, on the screen of which all manner of images are projected. It is seldom that we can control the nature of the pictures which may or may not have significance. The best the average person can do is to be on the alert to interpret the symbolic meaning of dream impressions when they come.

Whether dreams have dimension in and of themselves is an unanswered question. If they do, they exist in a time and space beyond our comprehension. At times they appear to have three-dimensional shape. Like a motion-picture film, they can occur in color or black and white. They can be fragmentary, presenting scenes in part or not in proper sequence. They can picture scenes that are grotesque and desolate, or landscapes of great beauty. usually in Subconscious response to the moods and feelings of the dreamer. They can produce fiendish monsters, fearsome snakes, and other threatening animals, as though instinctual relics of an awesome past. And, in contrast, they can bring to the dreamer illuminative, transcendent spiritual beings who inspire great faith and confidence that there must be a higher, finer plane of existence beyond this Life.

CHAPTER 9

The Power of Imagery in Spirit Communication

Imagery plays a vital part not only in mind-to-mind communication between living people but also between the minds of those who have left this life and those still on earth.

It has long been established that we think basically in pictures and that words are only the symbols of the images of whatever we have experienced. We must see these images in mind before we call upon words to describe them.

When the Chinese savanta said, "One picture is worth ten thousand words," they were testifying to the universality of pictorial communication—a simple power far beyond that of language—instantly comprehensible by all planetary peoples and all forms of intelligent life anywhere present or conceivable.

Space scientists have placed 116 pictures on board the Spacecraft Voyagers I and II now enroute on an endless journey past Jupiter, Saturn and countless stars beyond our galaxy. These pictures were carefully selected and recorded in electronic form. The sequence starts with a view of the solar system and moves to pictures of earth taken from space. Life is described with drawings of basic biology and pictures of a fetus, a birth, a nursing mother, a group of children and a family. Then there are pictures of a leaf, a snowflake, insects, fish, birds, elephants, and people of different races and cultures. To portray human technology, there are pictures of houses (African and New England) cities (Oxford and Boston), the United Nations building, and the Sydney, Australia opera house, a microscope, a radiotelescope, and a rocket launching.

Should some alien intelligent forms of life intercept and capture either Voyager I or Voyager II, a hundred thousand years from now or more, they can become acquainted with the nature of our civilization of long ago. Where any of us will be then is something to speculate upon! We hope wherever we are, if we are anywhere, that we will have evolved beyond our hates and prejudices and fears and our inhumanities to our fellow man and all life on our present troubled planet.

Of course we have tried to send the best pictures of ourselves out into space. We did not include any pictures of our starving, poverty-stricken, diseased masses in many countries, of our smog-ridden cities, our contaminated water supplies, our atomic wastes, our racial strife, and so on and on and on! If we had, and extraterrestrial creatures ever became possessed of this knowledge, it is doubtful if they would be inclined to visit us!

Perhaps, as wonderful as our planet still is with all Mankind has done to plunder its resources and despoil its natural beauties, this is the reason why many of us are hopefully picturing a more beautiful world, now invisible to us, in higher vibrating dimensions beyond, which we will experience when our life on earth is terminated.

Pictures! They have been with us from the moment of conception! The blueprint of the bodies we occupy today came into existence at that instant and the God-given creative power within faithfully followed this design as our bodies took form in our mothers' wombs.

We can't get away from our images. They are forming all the time as new experiences are coming to us. In ways we can perhaps never understand or explain, everything that happens in and around us is being photographed or recorded in some form by Nature—and our thought images continue to exist in what I call "the mental ether." A sensitive can often tune in on events that have happened and re-create the past of an experience as it is played back to him on the screen of his mind.

To one who can properly tune in to and interpret the movement of causative forces through time to their already determined effects—following the law of "like always attracting like"—the future can often be accurately read. That is IF—and this is a big IF—no stronger causative forces intervene or superimpose themselves upon the original causes and thus bring about an instant change in the potential effect.

Study this statement carefully—because a basic truth is contained therein!

Many people have heard of spirit mediums, but comparatively few have had opportunity to see and hear a genuine one in action. For this reason, our ESP Research Associates Foundation has presented Anne Gehman of Orlando, Florida, one of the country's finest psychics, in repeat appearances at our Annual Body, Mind, and Spirit Healing Workshop now held each year at the famous Chase Park Plaza hotel in St. Louis.

In recent times, there have been exposés of fraudulent mediums, and it is not wise for anyone to go to so-called psychics indiscriminately. No reputable psychic can guarantee in advance to receive verifiable impressions, and if he or she fails, it can be disappointing and even lead to a feeling, if one is inclined to be skeptical, that the medium is a fake.

Quite often, as in the case of my lifetime friend, Louis Spilman, a newspaper publisher from Waynesboro, Virginia, a person having a "sitting" may not recall incidents and names at the time, and may deny any truth in them.

Anne is always besieged with requests for appointments at the Workshop and has to decline most of them, but she made a special effort to accommodate the Spilmans for me.

During the "sitting" Anne told Louis that a tall man, with a moustache, named "George" wanted to get through to him. She got the impression he was a "shoemaker" or a "cobbler" . . . but Louis said he was sorry—this didn't mean anything to him.

Anne went on to say that this spirit wanted to thank Louis for what he had done for his loved ones. This didn't register with Louis. Then Anne turned to Emily, his wife, and said that Wilbur and John were there. They proved to be two deceased brothers of Emily's. John thanked Emily for what she had done for the family. Emily told us later that when John died, he left his family in difficult circumstances and she had given a check to the widow.

On the way home from the Workshop, Louis and Emily stopped off to see his half-sister. They told her of their psychic experience, and the half-sister said to Louis, "Why, Louis, don't you remember that our mother was married to my father, *George Shoemaker* . . . and that Anne, when she spoke of "shoemaking" was trying to give you his last name?" The half-sister said that her father was a tall man with a moustache.

Louis wrote Anne Gehman to apologize and said he didn't know how he could have been so stupid. He recalled that he had tried to be helpful to his half-sister, and George must have been trying to express his appreciation. Louis said he had never met his mother's former husband, George Shoemaker.

You can see from this how difficult it is for a spirit medium, in a public or even a private demonstration, to get confirmation for many of his or her impressions, at the time, which may cause many listeners to think they are more wrong than right. This is why psychics urge those to whom they are giving messages to please speak up, identify themselves when their name is mentioned or names of spirit entities, so contact can be maintained and a recognizable message delivered.

This case illustrates how the Subconscious mind of a sensitive, in trying to bring a message through, occasionally resorts to a symbolic image such as "shoemaker" which the medium's conscious mind must properly interpret. Had Louis Spilman been more acquainted with his mother's first marriage, of over eighty years ago, he could immediately have recognized the implication of the name "shoemaker." In checking Anne Gehman for possible accuracy, this could be scored as close to a direct hit.

The case histories to follow will all have a bearing on different means of communication where the power of imagery has been used to convey impressions. In some instances, there is evidence that more than imagery has been involved. Apparitions, defined as "a visual appearance of a disembodied spirit" have been seen, taking on seeming physical form, and in some instances actually speaking. Many times the person experiencing the visitation swears he or she was not asleep, that they were fully awake, although at other times these "spirit contacts" took place in dreams or a seeming out-of-body state.

One of the most unusual and convincing evidences of survival came about through the imagery received by a medium and reported to me by Dr. L. K. of Palos Verdes Estates, California. He writes:

Dear Mr. Sherman:
　With interest I read your book, *You Live After Death*. Answering your request to write you about the cases which support the hypothesis of "life after death," I have to describe to you the following:
　My very dear wife passed away five months ago. We loved each other so very much and I had several very colorful dreams since her death when I seemed to be with her—but dreams are dreams.
　Yesterday, however, I attended a symposium given by known medium, Freda Fell, from Canada (previously England). I never saw her. I did not even know anyone in the audience. At once, she interrupted her talk and looked at me. "Did you lose somebody near to you during the last couple months?" "Yes," I answered.
　"There is a lady here who shows me a ring . . . she

is your wife. . . . She said she was not suffering by
dying . . . and now she is okay—and very happy."

It was a big surprise to me. Because it stirred me so
deeply emotionally, I left the room. When the meeting
was resumed, she again said to me: "The lady is still
here. She says that January was the difficult month—the
operation. In February her parents from Yugoslavia
came and the sickness was getting better. In June, when
they left, the sickness turned worse, and at end of August,
she passed over, without pain.

"She shows me for some reason her hair—and asks
me to tell you it is now okay. She also says you have
someone playing the violin. She is very happy now . . .
she died from cancer. You can be assured she is here
with us."

I understand why she pointed to her hair. During her
sickness, due to medication, she lost her hair completely.
She was buried in a wig. Everything Freda Fell told me
was perfectly correct. There is no doubt that this medium
could not have known all the details . . . and certainly
nothing about myself. A friend of mine, an M.D. who
was present, was equally as surprised as I was. We both
are studying unusual psychic phenomana these last two
years. The *violin reference* had to do with my sister.

To me it proves that the soul not only survives, but
also found energy to come to me and to tell me she is
okay. You are right in your book when you state that
this is the law—and life has no borders or limits. Please
excuse me for my bad English—it is not my native language, and I do not have the time to correct this letter
with the dictionary.

Writes Mrs. L. M. of Fort Lauderdale, Florida:

"My husband and I lost our beloved daughter, Nellie,
just two months ago, at the age of one year and sixteen
days, although since her birth I had had repeated dreams
that she would die. I did not know how it would happen
and was not prepared for her tragic drowning in our
swimming pool.

The day that Nellie was buried, I sat on my bed,
crying and wishing that I could hold her just once
more . . . and I drifted off to sleep, with someone calling
my name. I awoke to find myself in a room not unlike

any room here except that it contained a huge desk. The man behind the desk asked me, "Who did you wish to see?" and I replied, "Nellie M." With this, he summoned her on what seemed to be a microphone, and she appeared. He told her she could visit with "her Mommy" for just a few minutes and then I would have to go. We did not talk but she climbed onto my lap, put her head on my shoulder, and laid there. It was only when I turned her around to gaze into her face that she slowly faded away, her body, which I felt as much as when she was alive, dissolved in my arms . . . and I was back in my bed. I don't know where I had been or how it could have happened, but I believe truly that God or some Higher Power had granted my wish . . .

(Note: This sounds as though Mrs. L. M. had a temporary out-of-body experience, reported by so many, when the two worlds of the living and the so-called dead seem to come together or fuse for the moment.)

. . . For some days after Nellie's passing, I asked Nellie, each night, before retiring, if she could ever forgive me for not watching over her more carefully and preventing her from drowning. I wished I could get some evidence that she heard me.

One morning, around 5 A.M. I heard a familiar noise coming from our patio. We have one of those electrical birds that chirps but it had been broken. This morning, however, it was chirping as loud as could be. It wasn't till later that morning that the realization came as we looked closely at Nellie's picture and saw on her dress— *a bird in a cage!*

Since this time, I have been in attunement with my daughter and she tells me everything she does. This is only through an inner voice, not through any other medium. One day, back in her room, I was looking at the table and chairs her father made for her, and started to cry. She asked me why I was crying and I told her it was because she could not play with her gift from Daddy. She started to laugh and told me that she plays with them every day . . . and that she has them with her. She also told me at that time what she wanted for Christmas and where I would find it.

I just believe that these things are too real to be my imagination, and I know in my heart that I can and have talked with my beloved Nellie.

More than an image is often seen when an actual life-like figure of a deceased friend or relative makes an unexpected appearance and is sometimes able to carry on a conversation. When this happens, it usually makes one wonder if it had, after all, been only a realistic dream, or a hallucination of some sort, or, impossible as it may seem, an out-of-body experience.

A Mr. R. C. of Hamilton, Ontario, Canada, had such a psychic adventure and after relating it, said:

What I would like to know is whether or not there are, in fact, dreams so seemingly real, or am I able to be detached from myself and wander about? If this is the case, is there any way to control this so it can be done at will? I have had more than one of these "dreams" where I found myself talking to people I know who have been long "dead." I am sending you a letter, along with this report on one of my experiences, from a friend verifying what I went through.

Mr. R. C. then narrated the following:

Some time ago a close friend of mine was killed in a car accident. He was a heavy drinker and was drunk at the time of the accident. At the time I was working in a local hospital on the night shift. About a week after the accident, I was in the lounge of one of the floors, dozing on my break, when my friend (the one killed) walked into the room and sat down and began talking to me. We talked about some of our times together and other trivia.

Then it dawned on me that he was dead! I mentioned this to him and he said that, yes, he was, but that he had been sent to warn me to give up my drinking or be prepared to face the same kind of death that he had faced.

I tried to ask where he was and how this was possible, but he refused to give me any information. I glanced away for a moment and when I looked back, he was gone. I immediately arose and went downstairs to tell of this incident to another friend, Miss S. J.

who is a believer in psychic phenomena. Here is her sworn statement as to what I told her.

Mr. R. C. referred me to a letter from this friend which he had enclosed. Here is her statement, in part:

Dear Mr. Sherman:
I am familiar with the contents of the preceding letter from Mr. R. C. since I typed it for him, and I can verify the facts as he has reported them. The night that the deceased friend came to visit, Mr. R. C. came to my office about 3:00 A.M. and was visibly shaken. He told me about the visitation, how real the experience had been. He was convinced that he was not sleeping at the time.

I have had psychic experiences of my own, so I know this can happen. Many years ago, my mother died suddenly. About two years after her death, I dreamed that I heard her voice and turned over (could I have still been asleep?) and she told me to get up and go to the kitchen immediately. Since there was such urgency to her voice, I did so, and found that the stove was still on beneath a pot of something or other. Had I not followed her instructions, I might well have died in the resulting fire. There have been many occasions when I have had the impression of seeing her out of the corner of my eye, but when I turned to look, there was no one. I be-believe that friends and loved ones are closer to us, many times, than we realize or are aware. Are these things my imagination? Am I dreaming, or what?

No, these people are not always dreaming. It is possible that images of spirit entities are received by the mind and are some way projected externally, like an image thrown on a screen by a motion picture projector. The unusual psychic, Ted Serios, has demonstrated under scientific testing, the ability to project images from his mind of such objects as the Statue of Liberty, the Eiffel Tower and other scenes and individual faces, which he impresses on sensitized film. He has turned the camera on himself, and instead of photographing his own features, entirely unrelated different images appear, images of things he is concentrating upon.

This is only one possible explanation of a variety of phenomena, and is not to say that the spirit entity itself is not present, at times, functioning as a result of its own energy forces, assembled and directed in a manner still unknown to us.

There is the case of Mrs. B. C. of Vacaville, California, who reported that she had been called from her home to Texas on April 12, 1974, to care for her father while her mother, ill with cancer, was in the hospital. Her mother, who had been in a coma for two months, died on May 2, but Mrs. B. C. remained with her father until May 20. She had been reluctant to leave him because, as she explained, her mother had waited on him hand and foot for over fifty years and he could not cook or even begin to know how to take care of the house. Mrs. B. C. relates:

On the night of May 18, 1974, I went to bed around 9:00 P.M. and I thought I was asleep when, all of a sudden, my mother appeared in the doorway, dressed in a green dress that I knew for sure was hanging in a closet in my brother's house. I asked her what she was doing there and she replied, "I can come and go as I please." I asked her what she was doing in that dress, as I knew it was at Homer's house in the closet. She answered, "I can wear anything I want to."

I then asked her what she wanted or what she was doing there and she said to me, "Go home. He will either stand on his own feet or fall flat on his face." After she spoke these words, she turned to leave. I tried to call her back because by this time I was sure I was not asleep. She made no reply and I have had no contact with her since then. My mother's appearance was one of happiness and health. She also looked younger than what she really was. I immediately made reservations the next morning to return to California, on May 20, and just explained to my father that I had to go home as I had a family that needed me. I related my experience to a friend of mine upon returning home. I have been careful not to tell many people as I figure most of them would think I was a little crazy. Thank you for letting me tell my experience to you.

Actually, some thousands of men and women have related similar experiences to me, through the years, and there is substantial evidence that, in critical or needful moments in their lives, departed friends or loved ones have returned in dreams or visions or seemingly actual visitations in an effort to be helpful or to warn of an impending death or accident or disaster, or to assure those on earth that they still live.

This does not necessarily mean that those in the After-life are endowed with an extensive knowledge of what is taking place on earth or what is going to occur in the future—and many people who have depended on the so-called messages and information received through psychics have been misguided and often disillusioned.

Generally, when direct and often unsought spirit communication comes to a person, as in some of these cases mentioned, it can be accepted as a genuine manifestation. We do not understand the conditions which have had to exist to make these psychic contacts possible—and why all people needful of some helpful communication or guidance are not so favored. Perhaps a partial explanation is that many people who might otherwise be reached by spirit friends or loved ones do not possess sufficient psychic sensitivity for those attempting communication to get through to their point of conscious awareness.

Here is one dramatic example of a case in which a spirit entity, anxious to reach a certain person, succeeded through a third party. It is told to me by Mrs. B. B. the woman who unwittingly served as the psychic channel.

I was sitting at my desk, at United Films, in Tulsa, working on some written material when, suddenly, a feeling came over me and seemed to fill the room. It was a presence that was so strong that I had to stop my work and try to understand what was happening. I sat quietly and relaxed. The clear impression of this girl, Lynn A., whom I had only met briefly ten years before, was right there in the room with me. I could not see her or hear an audible voice, but she was telling me that she was all right and everything was fine with her now, not to worry, and to tell everyone not to worry.

Lynn had been married to the curator of the Boston Museum for maybe fifteen years. They were having trouble, which wasn't unusual. She decided to come to Tulsa about six months ago, hoping to be reunited with her first husband. He is married and could not take her back. Deeply dejected because of her rejection, she returned to Boston, poured gasoline all over herslf, lit a match, and died a most horrible death. She had been quite a beautiful woman—intelligent, but emotionally unstable.

Her presence lingered about ten minutes with me in my office. Then Bill, my boss, came in, telling me to get my purse and note pad, that we were going to look at a building which might be suitable for a new studio. We arrived at the building and Bill introduced me to the real estate man, Mr. G. W. He said he had heard of me before through Bill, so we began talking. During the course of the conversation, he told me he had been married to Lynn, that he was her first husband. I was shocked, to say the least. I then told him that just fifteen minutes before, I had a vision of her and she told me everything was all right—that she was in a good place and to tell everyone not to worry about her. *He turned white.*

Then he told me that the night before, he was awakened out of a sound sleep, at which time her presence seemed to fill the room. There was no communication. He just felt her there, and he kept asking, over and over, where was she, how was she, was she all right? So here I come the next day with the answer to all his questions. He said he had never had such an experience before and had never been aware of her presence, except on this previous night.

Since I hardly knew the people involved and was completely unaware of a first husband, I felt this was a direct communication. His rejection of her had been, apparently, the last straw. She killed herself because of this and longstanding problems. She wanted to get word to him so she came through me, knowing I would be seeing him in the next few minutes. How marvelous is the Supreme Intelligence!

I asked Mrs. B. B. how she explained such a psychic experience coming to her, and she then confessed a most unusual practice of hers when she was a small child.

> When I was six or seven, my best friend's father owned the funeral home in Kirkwood, Missouri. We would have to pass it every day on the way home from school. Every day we would stop to say hello to her father, and I began the unusual practice of going to each casket where there was a corpse and holding each hand. I had no feeling of fear. I felt an overwhelming need to let them—each and everyone—know that there was someone who cared for them. I always felt such an incredible loneliness there—for them, not for me. No one ever seemed to visit, except me. At my young age, it just seemed that no one ever visited.
>
> It could be my great love for the dead souls at that age and even now is the reason they sometimes communicate through me.

It is usually difficult for people who have had no personal psychic experience in life to believe the reports of friends or loved ones such as are related here. If such an experience finally comes to them, it is often life-changing. The experiencer no longer wonders or guesses or doubts— and no one can any longer argue him out of it. Here is a case in point told me by Mrs. G. A. B.:

> I believe the most startling manifestation of mind's ability was on the evening following my grandmother's passing. She was my father's mother, a beautiful person who lived in my parents' home for so long as I can remember. I was eighteen at the time and had just given birth to my son, David, who is now five.
>
> I had just retired for the night when I became aware in my mind's ear of the roaring of ocean surf upon the beach and rocks. (As a very young child, and during the time of my most loved memories of my grandmother, we owned a resort motel in the small town of Cambria, California. The motel was located directly across the street from the ocean.)
>
> I turned to awaken my roommate and found I could not speak! My mouth was indeed open, but no sound at

all came forth. I then "saw" my grandmother in a beautiful light blue gown with white lace at the throat, as I had seen her in the casket at the funeral home. She spoke to me very clearly and distinctly. I should say I "heard" her in this manner; I cannot attest to remembering actually seeing her lips move. There was also a kind of "glowing" bright, white aura about her, not unlike an "energy field" of some sort.

She told me not to grieve, that she was happier than she had ever been. She was with her husband who had departed this world many, many years before, leaving her to grow to ninety-four years alone, and in great physical pain.

As I remember, she did "feel" the same to me. However, she had no wrinkles in her face, and her hands were no longer gnarled and ugly from arthritis. It was the most beautiful, wonderful experience I have ever had. After it, I found no reason to cry when witnessing her interment. This upset my family and I could not explain it properly. As the "vision" faded, so did the "roaring surf" and then—and only then—was I able to speak! Since then my belief in "beyond the senses" has continued to grow. This mind of mine and everyone's is a truly magnificent entity! I wish to do all I can to nurture and develop it.

From Mrs. G. A. B.'s description of this psychic experience, it is my feeling that she was temporarily out of her body and privileged to see images of another period in her life—even to hearing the "roaring of the surf"—as a means of establishing the reality of her grandmother's spirit presence.

What is called "materialization"—when spirit entities supposedly take form, usually in a séance room through the agency of a "materializing medium"—is a rare occurrence. There is perhaps no area of psychic phenomena which is faked more often. I have only seen one or two materializations during my entire life that I would rate as genuine. However, I have no reason to doubt that materialization can and does take place, and this detailed account given to me by George P. LaBorde of Salem,

Oregon, has the ring of authenticity to it. He presents it with this statement:

> I tell you this from the bottom of my heart. I have no intention of deceiving you or anyone else, but I am aware that you didn't see these things, and I don't expect you to believe them—but I *know!*
>
> The first materialization I ever saw was in San Francisco about thirty years ago. The medium was an older man, and the spirit forms were indistinct. Furthermore, I don't believe that the spirit entities were who they claimed to be.
>
> About ten years later, I attended a materialization séance in New Era, a Spiritualist camp some 30 miles north of Salem. The medium was Keith Rheinhart, at that time a young man of seventeen. There were thirty-three people in the room, which had no windows and only one door. No other rooms connected with it, and a piece of black cloth across one corner formed the "cabinet."
>
> Before the séance, he asked the ladies to come up and examine the "wall" of the cabinet. He then asked the men to step inside while he removed all his clothing to ascertain there were no "props" concealed. I was one who went up and was satisfied that what I saw later was genuine.
>
> There was a small electric bulb—about 7½ watts—which gave enough light so when our eyes became accustomed to the light, we could see readily. But what is much more important, there was a wooden box about 8″ x 8″ x 6″ over the door. There was an electric light in the box which was lighted and I guessed that might be as much as 25 watts. Anyhow, when it was on, the room was flooded with light, comparatively speaking.
>
> There was a movable shutter—I guess you would call it—which could be moved up and put the light out. There was no hook or other means of holding the shutter up and down, and there most certainly was no string or wire to move it up and down.
>
> Several times during the séance, when a particularly strong spirit materialized, the door to the little box would fly up and flood the room with light so we could see the spirit forms as clearly as we could see the people

around the room. Really, Harold, they were or seemed just as real as we people in the group.

One spirit claimed to be from the seventh sphere of heaven, or the Next Dimension, and as he came out of the cabinet, his voice just boomed out. I should tell you that each person in the group had three spirits materialize. This spirit took the arm of a little old lady in the circle and marched her around in front of the rest of us, while we all sang. He was dressed regally, and he conducted himself in a similar manner. He wore a gown and had a girdle about his gown which was just sparkling with jewels. My point now is that with the extra light, his presence was simply beyond doubt.

The medium's guide had told two men to station themselves in front of the cabinet, and as people were called to the cabinet, they were instructed to give a hand to each of these guards so that no one would be tempted to touch one of the materialized forms. When my turn came to approach the cabinet, the spirit of a Chaldean came out and told me to observe the color of his eyes. They were light blue, while the eyes of the medium were dark. I, for one, didn't need that assurance because I could see the medium sitting in his chair asleep. Anyhow, he told me to look into his eyes. I did, and they were really a beautiful light blue.

I should stop everything and interject right here that, as the séance neared its end, one of the guides asked me if there was anything more they might do to convince us. I replied, yes, there was. I had seen and heard these spirit entities. Now, would they touch me, to supply evidence of another sense. So I was told to come up and take each of the two guards' hands so I would not touch the spirit. I did as I was told and the spirit came close and slapped the back of my hand. I felt it and that convinced another of my senses. But I must add that after over half a century of experiences with mediums, I simply don't believe all I hear and see.

While I was just outside the cabinet, another spirit— a little girl—came out and told me to kneel down on one knee, so I did. As she came in front of me, laughing and happy, she said, "Watch me closely!" which I certainly did, and she grew up to full height right before my eyes. How she laughed at my consternation.

The third spirit that came out for me told me he was

going to do something special. I watched in amazement as he dematerialized in a sort of a whirlwind which became a tiny point of light—and then vanished.

Counting the medium's guides, I recall there were over 100 spirits which materialized that evening! One spirit told us that they did not lower their own vibrations—they raised ours instead, in order for us to be able to see and contact them. I am sure that this was so because I had the feeling of floating on air for several days after, and a most exhilarating sense of well-being.

So there is my account, and while I never expect to see such a demonstration again, I don't need to. I've seen it and am completely convinced.

If you are inclined to be skeptical, you might well question this extraordinary report by George P. LaBorde, despite his obvious sincerity and conviction. But what are you going to say about my friend, psychiatrist Elisabeth Kubler-Ross, who has publicly testified to having witnessed full-bodied materializations of not one, but three "spirit guides" in the presence of seventy-five people?

Dr. Kubler-Ross has gained recognition through her book *On Death and Dying,* which is based on her studies of over 1,000 people at the moment of death, who told of deceased relatives or friends who came to help them on their journey to the Hereafter. These people were revived after being pronounced clinically dead and returned with accounts of a beautiful life beyond. They stated that they had floated out of their bodies and had a sense of great peace, happiness, and beauty; they had not wanted to come back.

In December 1977 *Psychic News* (London) reported that Dr. Kubler-Ross lectured on the subject of "Life After Death" at a one-day seminar at the Seattle Opera House, to an audience of 2,500. She told of her contact with a group in Southern California which had been holding "materializing séances." Her account so impressed the audience that she was given a "prolonged standing ovation" for her courage in making her personal psychic experiences public.

According to *Psychic News,* Dr. Kubler-Ross returned

to her home in Flossmoor, Illinois, and was going through
a pile of several thousand letters, when she came upon
one from a group of people who had heard her express a
belief that a guide or "guardian angel" accompanies each
person through life. At their meetings they had prayed
that their guides would be revealed to them. These prayers
had been granted. If Dr. Ross would meet them on a certain day, her own guide would materialize.

Then came a strange coincidence. She was about to
reject the offer when her phone rang. Dr. Kubler-Ross
discovered she would be in that Southern California town
to meet a group of physicians on the same day. She therefore accepted the strange invitation "provided 75 impar-
tial witnesses could be found to attend the proceedings,
and that there would be enough light for any manifestations to be clearly seen. In addition, a taped recording
must be made."

The group agreed to these conditions. *Psychic News*
continues:

> Then, to the doctor's amazement, a seven-foot figure
> materialized in front of her, spoke for a time, and then
> disappeared into the floor.
> Then, to use her own words, "a handful of ectoplasm
> appeared and, growing, was transformed into a tall
> Egyptian who announced he was her special guide who
> had been with her since birth." She could feel his touch,
> as, cupping his hands under hers, he led her out of the
> room and into a nook where they were able to talk
> privately about her life's work. Then he led her back
> into the room, where his visible form disintegrated be-
> fore the eyes of the group and the seventy-five witnesses.

But more was to come. There appeared a third guide,
complete with a clipped beard. When this remarkable test
séance ended and others left, Dr. Ross told two or three
group members who lingered that she longed to see her
special guide under more intimate circumstances. Would
he be able to materialize again?

It was possible—and all three guides reappeared. The

first two, including the Egyptian, spoke briefly. Then all three dematerialized once more, seeming to dissolve into the floor.

Following this first meeting, a psychic development came to Dr. Kubler-Ross so that she was able to provide the energy for her guide to appear to her almost at will. She claims she has since seen him a hundred times or more and has scores of tape recordings of conversations she has had with him which are being prepared for public record.

Says Dr. Kubler-Ross:

This is not a rare phenomenon anymore. It can be created by the right group of people who have no fear and no negativity, who pool their energies together for the purpose of communicating with their visible and very physically present guides. We have been able to materialize our spirit guides, to be in their physical presence, to touch them, to sing with them, to record their teachings, to ask for advice, and even to share a sense of humor with them.

Dr. Ross is aware of the price she may have to pay for saying these things. "I can lose everything I've ever worked for my whole life," she said. "But if I had any doubts, I would keep them private." Through supportive friends, she has established a "healing center" to be opened on 40 acres, north of Escondido, California. It is to be called Shanti Nilaya, which means "home of peace." It is a place where terminally ill and dying patients may come, with relatives and friends, and who may be spiritually prepared to make the transition into the "next life."

I cannot personally testify, as yet, to the validity of these materializations, but I know that such a phenomenon does exist. And I have great respect and regard for Dr. Kubler-Ross and the great contribution she is making to the removal of the fear of death.

A heart-touching letter came to me some time ago from Mrs. G. Y. of Pittsburgh, Pennsylvania. She wrote:

My first experience with psychic phenomena occurred about six weeks after my little boy was killed. Perhaps I ought not to think that, because on the morning before the tragedy, I heard "Honey" talking to his two-year-old sister. Apparently there was a little friction between them, for he said, "I don't care. Anyway, I'm going to God soon."

The following day was Palm Sunday. My small daughter had started down the stairs. She began to fall when Honey ran up the stairs and caught her. "Pat," he said, "Be careful. Someday I won't be here to catch you."

The previous night, I had dreamed that he, who was seldom naughty, had annoyed me. I had chased him into my bedroom and he went through the second-story window and disappeared.

A man traveling so fast that his car skidded 70 feet going up hill on a dry day, struck my little boy. He picked him up, brought him into my bedroom, and laid him on the bed. Honey was gone in ten minutes.

Six weeks later, when my neighbor of Jewish faith called on me, we sat with our backs to the windows facing the fireplace. There was an archway in the hall which led to the bedroom. In the archway, I saw a misty form in the shape of Honey. I turned to my neighbor and said, "Mrs. Gould, you are going to think I am queer but—" She interrupted me and said, "Did you just see Honey? I saw him as plainly as could be."

That evening I asked my husband to take me to hear a spirit medium who purported to be clairaudient and clairvoyant. We listened to requests to locate lost rings and other material requests and questions. I whispered, "Leland, let's leave." We were about to stand when Mr. Cutter said, "I want to go to someone who has two grandmothers standing beside her, both named Elizabeth." I did not feel that the statement was directed to me because my grandmother was Harriet, though Leland's grandmother was Elizabeth. (Months later, I learned from my mother that my grandmother was named Elizabeth Harriet Littlefield, though we had called her Hattie.)

Mr. Cutter continued, "There is a little boy here

holding out his hands, and in them is a little bunny.
You buried it with him."

I had bought the children plush bunnies for Easter,
and before the undertaker closed the casket, *I had picked
up his bunny and tucked it in beside him.*

With what we considered as proof of his continued
existence, we have not seen or heard from Honey since.
We have felt that he should be allowed to go on and not
be held back by our selfishness.

This account of Honey, his premonitions of his own
coming transition, his apparitional appearance, and the
image of himself and his bunny which he transmitted
through the medium, caused me to think of my beloved
brother, Edward Sherman, who fell from a tree in our
front yard in Traverse City, Michigan, broke both arms
so badly that tetanus set in, and died a week later.

As death was approaching, Edward was conscious, but
his eyesight failed. He said, "I can't see you—can you
see me?" We assured him that we could. He had no fear,
but his vision seemed to go beyond this life as he lifted
little broken arms and reached out and said, "You . . .
you!" He "saw" his Aunt Flora and Cousin Lillian,
bound for Traverse City by train from Marion, Indiana,
as though they were there, though he had not been told
of their coming.

He then knew he was going and, puckering up his
fevered lips, said, "Kiss you . . . kiss you," and told all
in our little family circle—father, mother, brother Arthur
and me good-bye. He then seemed to hear heavenly
music and tried to hum it. His suffering that week had
been agonizing, but he had borne it manfully. Then he
passed on with his sightless earth eyes fixed on scenes we
could not perceive.

"Edward," so the neighbors said, "was too fine a soul
to have lingered long with us."

I wrote Mrs. G. Y. and told her that her experience
with Honey had brought back the sacred memory of my
brother, to me. And I said to her, I knew what a joy it
would be to her to meet her son, one day, again, as it

would be a joy for me to meet my brother Edward, both boys now long since matured to full manhood in this life we are still to experience.

What consoling images for so many of us to carry who share the conviction that death is not the end, but only a new beginning.

CHAPTER 10

The Power of Imagery in Television

Never before, in the known history of the world, has an invention had such an impact on human consciousness as television! The influence of motion pictures has been powerful enough, but when an instrument brought PICTURES into every home, available without restriction to people of all ages, and particularly the impressionable minds of young children, the EFFECT on their physical, mental, emotional, sexual and spiritual nature was profoundly life-changing!

For a time, lost in the fascination of this new medium of communication, doctors, psychiatrists, sociologists, educators, police authorities, parents and responsible persons in all walks of life did not realize the enormous potential it was creating for evil as well as good.

"The fact is," said a concerned TV commentator, "that television's dependence on pictures (and the most vivid pictures) makes it not only a *powerful* means of com-

121

munication but a *crude* one which tends to strike at the emotions rather than at the intellect. For TV journalism this means an increasing concentration on action (usually violent and bloody) rather than on thought, on happenings rather than on issues, on shock rather than on explanation, on personalities rather than on ideas. TV can cover a riot, a war, a revolution, an assassination more vividly than any newspaper; but it also tends to give much less impressive treatment to the reasons behind these events. . . . The insatiable appetite of television for dramatic, action-packed pictures has wide and profound implications. What is TV doing to the minds of its viewers, young and old? What has it already done?"

Today, experts in the fields of psychiatry and psychology are warning that "Many TV shows are leading viewers to believe that the only way to achieve goals in life is through lying, cheating, fraud, violence and sex, and that young people can take the law into their own hands. Even the good guy has to use violence rather than his intelligence to overcome the bad guy, which constitutes a new low in TV programming.

"In some TV shows it is all right to beat up a person, or even kill him to gain your end. As for sex, it's a matter of who sleeps with whom and who can cut whose throat. This plants the seed in young people's minds that living together is the accepted practice and the only way to make out is to be totally ruthless in professional and personal relationships. Heroes are not always good people—they lie and connive and literally get away with murder. The way to assume leadership is through physical violence and defiance of authority."

Every hour of the day and night, the mind is fed a pictorial diet of often unsavory and highly suggestive images which many human systems cannot digest. They play upon feelings of anger, resentment, jealousy, frustration and the like until the pent-up emotions of some individuals explode into acts of uncontrolled sex and violence.

"There is no doubt that television coverage causes imitation," is a conclusion that is being voiced by more and more psychiatrists and police authorities. "Children especially, are born imitators and often try to enact in real life what they see on the television screen. Their minds are constantly filled with images of those who kill and murder and maim and torture and rape; who perform all manner of sex acts, or suggest them; who commit sabotage and other savage acts of destruction; who defy parental guidance, and who spew hate and feelings of revenge. All this, unhappily under commercial sponsorship."

War is glorified and viewers see actual humans riddled with bullets or blown to pieces by bombings in the name of self-defense. Criminals and dope-addicted, crazed men and women, holding innocent hostages at gun or knife or bomb point, become actors before audiences numbering into the millions. The TV camera is made to plead the causes of political dissidents who hijack planes and people in cars or buses or in business houses or homes—under threat of destruction or death.

While many commercial sponsors, defending their highly rated TV programs, will argue that violence and sex on TV does not inspire violence and sex in real life, the evidence is overwhelming that those who are actual or potential child molesters and rapists are stimulated by pornographic films and TV programs featuring glamorous sex scenes and sadistic or masochistic acts of violence.

Many sex offenders have admitted that their assaults were triggered by TV scenes and motion pictures which they have relived and reviewed in their minds, magnified by their own sexual desires, until a compulsion drove them to seek an enactment of their lurid visualizations against their victims.

They expressed no remorse for their acts, since they had pictured some other entity inside them taking over and performing the misdeed. As one of them said, when under a death sentence for molesting hundreds of boys and killing seven, "I would kill again if I am freed. I have done it for thrills. . . . I have absolutely no feeling whatsoever for any of the boys I murdered, or for their parents either. I rejoice every time I hear a little boy being murdered. I can't be changed. Everybody hates me . . .

so the sooner I am electrocuted, the better. Maybe then the Lord can change me."

But the minds that are most damaged by the imagery of television, even though there are good, entertaining and instructive shows, are the minds of children, beginning at an early age and continuing on up to young adulthood. They are brainwashed into developing a taste and a liking for various food and drink products; into preference for certain toys, novelties, sporting equipment, cars, and clothing—you name it! When you sell the child on anything, you have more than half sold the parent.

A child expert, in denouncing what he termed "unethical TV commercials," said, "These commercials make kids respond like puppets on a string, who dance to the tune of the advertisers. They start clamoring for products in return for the gimmicks offered and the instant popularity that possession of these products promises. It is possible to plant a string of words or pictures into a child's mind so that they will be remembered for years and years."

More dangerous than these commercially designed ways for influencing a child's mind are the highly emotional TV shows themselves which excite the child and cause him to impulsively seek to duplicate what he has seen. For example: two children jumped from a roof—they were playing "Batman." Another child set his house on fire, copying an arson incident he saw on TV. The list could be extended almost endlessly. The moral and ethical effects can hardly be estimated.

Why paint such a grim picture? Why not emphasize the great educational contributions of television, its universal capacity for reaching and influencing all minds? This is just the reason! Television is an absolutely gigantic two-edged sword. It can and does cut both ways—dependent on the nature of the images on the cutting edge.

Today educators, parent-teacher associations, psychiatrists, doctors, and other responsible elements of Society are expressing growing concern over the demoralizing aspects of certain types of TV programs. They are trying to curb or greatly reduce the number of lurid pictures of violence and sex on motion picture and TV screens by letters of protest to government leaders and heads of TV networks, and by boycotts of sponsors' products, as well as public condemnation.

The situation is already out of hand, and the problem is too enormous to be dealt with in any of these ways. Where profits are involved, any attempt to curtail or change the nature of pictures or programs which are making money for producers or manufacturers will be fought strenuously. And the show people have a point: when "respectable" family pictures have been made, few have been successful at the box office or on TV. The general public has been so conditioned to accept blood and thunder, sex-sated and disaster pictures that gentle, romantic domestic pictures have usually had little or no appeal.

The stark facts are, of course, that life itself is filled with violence. Producers can therefore claim that they are just reflecting life as it is, rather than contributing to the violent conduct of people. On the surface, there would seem to be merit to this contention. A fire may have been started by other causes, but fuel can be poured on the fire from other sources—and television coverage of personal and world events, in fact and fiction, has not only been keeping the fire going, but fanning it into a conflagration!

What's to be done about it? Very little can be done directly. What is imperatively needed is a massive educational program, established in all school systems, beginning with young children and continuing on up through adult life—so that every person will clearly understand how his mind operates and what he is doing to himself by wrong thinking.

What man must be brought to realize is that he is exactly what he has PICTURED himself to be. This fundamental fact must be repeated over and over again. There is no getting around it—you are what you have pictured or will picture. No change of any consequence can take place in your life until and unless you remove the wrong pictures from consciousness and replace them with positive images for your creative power to work on.

It would be advisable, therefore, if things haven't been going right in any department of your life, to ask yourself: "What is wrong with my picture?"

You can't live in this world of sensation and violence without being influenced by the images of what goes on about you. At any age, you are bound to become involved to a greater or lesser degree, depending on your position in life. You can't escape it. It is not enough that man is causing his self-destruction by polluting air, earth, and water, but even more dangerous—he is also permitting the pollution of his own mind.

Amid all this, it has to be said, Television is the great Frankenstein monster. It can make or break any individual or any product if it presents the wrong picture of a person or object. All the elements of good and bad are contained in it. Each broadcast image becomes the blueprint for like impulses and actions on the part of many viewers, especially impressionable young people whose minds are not so capable of distinguishing the real from the unreal, truth from fiction, and who accept what they see as a way of life or something that should be experimented with or imitated.

Every picture is like a seed planted in the soil of your Consciousness. If it is nourished by your desires or fears, it begins to take on a life of its own and to blend with other images of like nature, seeking manifestation in some form in your outer life.

How deeply you feel for or against an image of a person, an advertised product, or an idea determines the degree of its influence upon you at any given time. All images in your mind are ready to respond on an instant's notice, magnetized into action as your attention is attracted or directed to them.

Whatever you give reality to in your mind, whether it is imagined or an actual experience, becomes an indistinguishable part of you. If the images are of a disturbed and distorted nature, they cannot change as long as you continue to harbor them with similar thoughts and feelings.

Those who desire to influence and control the thinking of great masses of people know the power of *picturization*, know how to arouse strong feelings for or against a situation or an issue, how to make people think what they want them to think—unless these people are awake and aware of this approach.

You do not have to accept the PICTURES that are being bombarded at you! If your mind is free of fears, worries, hates, prejudices, and other destructive thoughts, it will recognize these wrong pictures wherever and whenever encountered, and you can reject them—refuse to let them become a part of your Consciousness.

You cannot avoid exposure to programs which tend to disrupt or destroy family life by picturing the glamorous position of women outside the home as compared to the unexciting and unrewarding duties of a wife and mother, committed to the routine demands of sewing, cooking, and ordinary housework. Those who are living together, enjoying premarital and extramarital sex, or engaged in homosexual or lesbian practices, are often cast in implied, enticing favored roles, which many viewers are tempted to emulate.

Ask yourself if you seem to be susceptible to any one or more of these images. If you are, you may be taken in, either in whole or in part, on occasion, without your realizing it at the time.

Many men and women, in recounting disturbing experiences, have said to me: "I know I shouldn't have done it, but I couldn't help myself. He (or she) overwhelmed me. I couldn't say no. I didn't seem to have any will of my own. I was flattered into feeling I was a god in the making, and I was ready to make any sacrifice of money, even relatives and friends, to become all powerful. I lost all sense of judgment. The personal as well as the sex appeal was too strong. I felt like a different person."

People so moved may not have been drinking, under the influence of drugs, or "turned on" through use of psychedelic chemicals, although one or more of them is usually a contributing factor. In the presence of mind pollution, an individual can be influenced to commit indiscreet acts simply through lack of mental and emotional stability, an urge that has been permitted to get out of bounds. The mental images associated with strong feelings build up into demands for outlet or expression that will not be denied regardless of circumstances or consequences.

You are safe from the invasion of any emotionally charged images which might influence you against your will, so long as you are able to maintain control of your own feelings. But the moment you permit some imagery aimed at you to take over and dominate your feelings, you lose all reason and lay yourself open to forces outside yourself which can move in and cause you to do things you would not normally do.

It is not possible to fully protect the mind of a child. Parents can refuse permission to look at certain television shows and try to keep him from viewing a late-night program or certain programs which are advertised in advance as not suitable for juveniles, but the child will manage to see some of these programs regardless. He is also exposed to pornographic literature and pictures, picked up at school or in neighborhood book and magazine store racks. In most cases, parental disapproval is ineffective. The curiosity of most children and their desire for experimentation will enable them to make discoveries and observations of knowledge which their elders may have tried to keep from them.

Hopefully, the average parent is not involved in practices which would cause him or her to instruct the child: "Don't do as I do, do as I say." An example of right living and right thinking is the best deterrent to a child's tendency at misconduct. His image of loving attitudes of parents toward each other and toward himself is usually the greatest protection that could be given.

More than that, if parents and others charged with the responsibility of informing and educating children could give them a simple explanation of the power of their own minds to attract whatever they picture for themselves in time, a child could judge what he is doing or desiring to do, and could guard himself against the influence of imagery he knows would be harmful.

Of course, many young people, so warned, will still want to try to experience—at least once—and run the risk of getting hooked because they will want to repeat what gives pleasure. This is human nature. It is animal nature. It is all nature. Men and women in increasing numbers are playing games with LSD and other psyche-delic drugs. They are looking for other worlds, ultimate realities. They want to cry, they want to laugh, they want to scream, they want to suffer or they want to torture, they want to deviate, they want to be born again from the womb, they want to be a drop of water in the ocean of life, they want to change their sex, they want to be great poets, and writers and composers, they want to escape the domination of the senses, they want the inner peace that is beyond comprehension, they want to taste the liquors of life, they want to kill, they want to commit suicide, they want to be one with the Infinite, one with God, they want the most tremendous of all experiences: they want to *be* God!

Characteristic with most of humanity, men and women tend to follow the path of least resistance. Instead of mak-ing a sustained, conscious effort for self-development, to activate the higher powers of the mind, aimed at eventually experiencing transcendental adventures in consciousness, they are seeking mind expansion and greater sensual pleasures by the shortcut methods of hypnosis, electronic and chemical devices.

Young people are rebelling against everything that they consider orthodox, conventional, regimented, stuffy, re-pressive or inhibiting in society. "Youth wants to know" is a phrase that is often bandied about, and youth contends it cannot know unless it is given a free hand to explore life on its own.

Having observed what a mess some of their elders and parents have made and are making of the present-day world, youth is taking bizarre and violent means to dem-onstrate its disapproval and discontent.

To many, morality is becoming amoral; religion, irre-ligious; self-expression, unpredictable and explosive; per-sonal behavior, more and more individualistic and defiant. This is not to say that all of this is necessarily bad. It may eventually lead to a new kind of stability if the people, now in a state of shock to the point of helpless indifference, are able to keep a basic faith in government and business afloat against the seeming never-ending flood of Watergates.

And Television, because of its intimate contact with the minds and emotions of Youth, pictures many of the scenes and activities in which Youth feels it wants to participate. It beats the drum of life, and Youth responds to it as though one would follow a Pied Piper.

Each day you should guard against pollution of your mind through the conscious or unconscious acceptance of wrong images permeating the very atmosphere, directed at you from practically every medium of communication, especially Television. You now know how your mind operates, how mental pictures are created, as well as received by you, and what can happen to you, in time, if wrong thoughts and feelings are harbored in your Subconscious.

You and you alone are responsible for what you think and how you feel about things. What you think and feel, multiplied by what everyone else on this planet thinks and feels, is going to determine not only your future, but theirs!

Your mind, rightly controlled and directed, can make you one of the finest, most successful, best-liked individuals on earth.

CHAPTER 11

The Power of Imagery in Sports

In my school years I was active in sports—particularly baseball, basketball and tennis. When I began my writing career, I wrote sport stories and novels for men and boys and became one of the outstanding juvenile authors of that day. In the 1920s and 1930s, many of my stories appeared in *Boys' Life Magazine,* the official publication for the Boy Scouts of America. I ended up with over sixty sport novels to my credit—on baseball, basketball, football, ice hockey, track, and tennis, which sold into the hundreds of thousands of copies. Of course, they are now long since out of print, but I am often asked in my question and answer period, following my lectures on ESP and the higher powers of the mind: "Are you the same Harold Sherman who wrote those sport stories I read as a boy, or my dad used to read?" Such is the flight of time!

Even in those early days, I had discovered the power of visualization, and was practicing it as a baseball pitcher

131

and center fielder, as a forward on the basketball teams, and as a player on the tennis court. I found that if I pictured in my mind what I wanted to accomplish, before I acted, that I was much more effective in every physical movement I made. Today this power of visualization is widely used and being taught by instructors in different sports.

In my day, there were few uniform backboards on basketball courts. Most of them were made of wood; glass or composition backboards were not yet in style. There was a different resiliency to the wood, and the bounce of the ball off these backboards differed, so if you aimed at a certain spot on one backboard, it did not carom into the basket at just the same angle, as off other backboards. Most players, however, banked their shots into the basket off the backboards. Not too many shot for the rim.

I hit upon the idea—not original with me—of aiming at the basket and avoiding the backboard as much as possible, from whatever position I was in on the court. As I practiced, picturing the trajectory I would need to launch the ball to drop it through the hoop without touching the rim, I greatly increased the percentage of hits.

One of my pet shots was a position I placed myself in, in the right or left corner of the court, just inside the line beyond the basket, where you had to shoot for the rim because you could hardly hit the backboard. It was an angle that was often unguarded, so as I took a pass from a teammate, I had a split second more to picture the arch of the ball. As I saw and sensed what a push it would take to follow this arch in my mind's eye, I released the ball . . . and if I released it at the very moment I saw this picture, my muscular reaction projected the ball unerringly through the hoop. I could tell the instant the ball left my hands if it was going in or not.

In the excitement of a game, if I could manage to keep my nerves under control and remain unhurried as I got the ball and eyed the basket, and took a "snapshot" picture in my mind of the loop it would require to hit the basket from wherever I was on the floor, my muscles propelled it in just the right arch—and in it went!

When I played, the basketball rules permitted a team to have a "sharpshooter" to go to the foul line whenever anyone was fouled. Today, of course, the player who is fouled does the shooting. But I had gained the reputation of a "dead eye" at the foul line and seldom missed. If I took my time and visualized the path the ball should take to drop through the hoop, I often scored, hardly swishing the net.

Everyone today who plays basketball or who sees it played is familiar with the hoop shot which almost every basketballer uses. One witnesses exciting games of college and professional teams on television where one spectacular shot after another is made from all points on the floor, the ball scarcely touching the rim. The players have become split-second visualizers—a quick look—aim at the basket—an instant follow-through as soon as the picture is completed . . . and swish—two more points!

It is generally only the close-up shots where the ball is banked off the backboard. Dunk shots don't count, of course—and I wish they weren't allowed. There is little art in jumping up and jamming the ball into the net. And height of a player is often a substitute for finesse.

After all these years, and now living on 200 acres in the wilds of these beautiful Ozark hills I have installed a basketball backboard against a backstop of trees in our front yard. It has provided me with excellent exercise, but, more importantly, it has enabled me to keep a fine edge on my visualizing.

Whether you are sports-minded or not—and most of us are these days—you are controlled, as I have stated again and again, by the kind of images you create in mind of whatever goal, large or small, you have in life. Everything you do must be pictured before you do it, even if it is only putting a ball through a hoop.

Take baseball. It applies to any position you play but, in my case, I played as a pitcher or outfielder. It happened that I broke my right wrist when I was six years old. I was naturally right-handed, but the arm did not heal rapidly and I did everything left-handed for some months, so I became ambidextrous. In high school, while I favored my left hand for pitching, I was able, on occasion, to shift to my right hand in pitching to a left-handed batter. In tennis, I wielded the racket with my right hand mostly, but I could shift to my left hand to hit balls ordinarily out of reach. This all required constant visualizing, to direct my attention from one arm to the other. This injury to my arm at this early age proved to have been a "good break."

On the pitching mound, I would size up the batter—study his stance at the plate, whether he crowded the plate or stood back—and pictured in my mind just where to throw the ball to make it most difficult for him to hit. The catcher would take head signals from me as to where to hold his mitt as a target; high or low, wide or close.

Once I had decided on where to pitch, I took a few seconds to take mental aim at the mitt. I was unmindful of the sounds of the crowd or attempts of rival team members to upset me—and if I could maintain this concentration, the ball would usually go to the visualized objective.

In the outfield, I would move to the right or left, go farther out or come in closer to the diamond as different batters came to the plate, relying either on my sensing of where to place my self or any directions I got from our pitcher or catcher.

When a ball was hit to my field, I would take one look at its flight and, if over my head, picture about how far I would need to turn and run in order to get under the ball before making the catch. Experience had taught me how to do this, but an intuitive sense told me each time about how far to run and to the right or left before looking back, again sighting the ball and getting under it.

What I was doing is what every athlete has to learn to do, whether he or she realizes the mechanics of it or not. We are picturing, in one way or another, every waking moment of our lives.

Football is a game I have never played, but I have written many novels about it, one of them dealing, in fictional form, with the gridiron exploits of one of football's immortals, the great Red Grange, the Galloping Ghost of Illinois, It was titled *One Minute to Play* published in 1926, and was made into one of the first feature pictures on sport ever produced, with Red Grange, who had turned professional, as the star. The book came out simultaneously with release of the picture and sold into the hundreds of thousands of copies. Then I, as the young author of *One Minute to Play* was engaged by Dailey Paskman, manager of radio station WGBS, New York, to broadcast one of the first running descriptions of a football game, when Red Grange made his professional football debut as a member of the Chicago Bears, playing against the New York Yankees in Yankee Stadium. Red was noted for his amazing open-field running. Once his teammates could break him through the line, he was usually gone for long gains or a touchdown. Few opponents were able to lay hands on him.

With the help of the press, Red established the image in the minds of the public, as well as opposing players, of an almost uncatchable, unstoppable running back. In his professional career, people came to the game expecting electrifying performances. In many instances, they were not disappointed. Sports fans never tired recounting how Red, playing for Illinois against the most powerful Michigan team in history, scored four touchdowns the first four times he got his hands on the football, dodging and twisting and reversing his fields, as he ran through a team of frustrated Michigan players, left diving and tackling thin air.

Yes, the right kind of imagery in any sport has terrific impact. Each member of a football team has to carry the image in mind of the part he is trained to play in whatever position he is assigned. He must see an instant picture of each play as it is called and what he is supposed to do when the play is executed. In real life, it is not always possible to carry out what we visualize because of opposing forces or some failure to perform, but everything must start with an image, a goal, an objective.

My ESP Foundation associate, Al Pollard, who played years ago on the University of Arkansas football team, told me of a time when they were playing a losing game. He was getting more and more aroused as the opposing team was pushing down the field toward the Arkansas goal. He recalls that, while he was only one member of the team, he pictured himself breaking through the enemy line from his backfield position and hitting the quarterback so hard that it would knock the ball out of his hands—and he would scoop up the ball and run up the field for a touchdown.

With this emotionally powerful picture in mind, he somehow gathered almost superhuman strength, vaulted the opposing line, crashed into the quarterback, saw the ball spin out of the quarterback's hands, pursued it, grabbed it up and kept on running in the open field until he went over the line for the touchdown he had visualized.

Of course, this couldn't happen every time; but this successful enactment of what he had pictured was undeniably the result of a planned maneuver on his part. Quite often, one does not stop to realize that what he has done or not done has been the outgrowth of what has first been pictured.

Golf is another game I have never played. I presume it's because, in later life, I never felt I had a half a day or a day's time to chase a little ball over hill and dale and in and out of sand traps or water holes. But golf today has become one of the great national pastimes as well as a big money sport.

One of my sports-loving friends is Jack Scott, an athlete who is teaching what he calls "Visual Golf" at a golf club in Tempe, Arizona. Jack started years ago practicing "how to picture what he wanted" from reading different books of mine, among them *The New TNT-Miraculous Power Within You*. He has applied this technique of thinking to the game of golf, and all top golfers as well as duffers are using it: surveying every lie before each stroke, picturing just what club to use, just how hard to hit the ball, just where they want it to land or how far to roll.

The synchronization of body movement with mental picturing is the name of every game. The power of imagery in sport, as in everything else you do in life, is not to be discounted. You are calling upon it all the time—but are you conscious of doing it and taking full advantage of its possibilities? If not, start giving thought to how you can better your imagery and, consequently, your performance.

CHAPTER 12

The Power of Imagery in Creativity

The CREATIVE POWER OF MIND is the CREATOR'S greatest gift to man. Without this IMAGINATIVE faculty—the ability to PICTURE what you want—without the capacity of this Creative Power to MAGNETICALLY attract what you want, good or bad, nothing could come into existence. We have been given all the ingredients and elements with which to work, but we must first PICTURE what we want to put the force of CREATION into operation.

An inspiring illustration of this unalterable fact is contained in this article written by Dr. Allen A. Stockdale, which appeared quite some years ago in an issue of *Christian Economics*:

GOD LEFT THE CHALLENGE IN THE EARTH

When God made the Earth, He could have finished it.

But He didn't. Instead, He left it as a raw material—to set us thinking and experimenting and risking and adventuring! And therein we find our supreme interest in living.

Have you ever noticed that small children in a nursery will ignore clever mechanical toys in order to build, with spools and strings and sticks and blocks, a world of their own imagination?

And so with grown-ups, too. God gave us a world unfinished, so that we might share in the joys and satisfactions of CREATION.

He left the oil in Trenton rock.

He left the electricity in the clouds.

He left the rivers un-bridged—and the mountains un-trailed.

He left the forests un-felled and the cities un-built.

He left the laboratories un-opened.

He left the diamonds un-cut.

He gave us the challenge of raw materials—not the satisfaction of perfect, finished things.

He left the music un-sung and the dramas un-played.

He left the poetry un-dreamed, in order that man and woman might not become bored, but engage in stimulating, exciting, creative activities that keep them thinking, working, experimenting and experiencing all the joys and durable satisfactions of achievement.

PROGRESS comes, not by some magic work and not by government edict—but from the thoughts, the toil, the tears, the triumphs of individuals who accept the CHALLENGE of RAW MATERIAL—and by the grace of GOD-GIVEN talents produce RESULTS which satisfy the needs of men.

Every new thought, every experience is a challenge. We have the power to create what we want out of the opportunities which come to us or which we can make for us, dependent on our attitude of mind.

"Are You Using Your Brains?" This is a question asked by Dr. Whitt N. Schultz of Kenilworth, Illinois, to who I am indebted for this statement:

You have billions of brain cells.
In fact, your brain has the remarkable capacity to

take in, process, program and utilize more than 600 memories per second for 75 years (and more!) That's 51,840,000 bits of intelligence per day that your mental computer can handle!

Are you using your brain—and the brains all around you?

You—and every other normal person—have four brain powers: They are:

Your absorptive brain power—That's the power to take in knowledge through the "gateways to your mind," your senses. Open up your mind. Let the sunshine in!

Your retentive power—This is your memory. Stored in your "library of knowledge" is everything you have experienced in your lifetime, up until now.

Your judgmental power—Your power to judge, to make choices, to respond to situations based on your facts (which are often incomplete) This power is usually so active that it gets in the way of . . .

Your imaginative power. This is the tremendous strength of your imagination. As youngsters, our imaginations were alert and utilized constantly. But unfortunately, throughout the years, our imaginative powers were stifled by what I call "killer phrases"—"It won't work" . . . "It's not in the budget" . . . "We tried that before and it doesn't work!" "No way," etc., etc.

It's the great growing and mostly unused power of the imagination which most business people fail to generate. And yet today, if ever there is a time to use our imaginations to come up with solutions, that time is now.

One way to generate renewed mind power is to bury forever the Laurence J. Peter "Peter Principle." You know that theory: "In a hierarchy every employee tends to rise to his level of incompetence."

Hogwash! No manager should accept that theory. It's true that one of the tragedies of American corporate life is that many employees who haven't, so to speak, "made it" by the time they are 40, feel all washed up.

Nonsense! A recent study of industrial history shows many a corporation wouldn't be around today if its founder felt he was finished by the time he reached 40 years of age.

Here are a few examples to illustrate the point:

At 40, R. H. Macy already had four unsuccessful flyers at storekeeping. His fourth venture ended in bankruptcy.

Still he had guts to try again. The fifth venture paid off—big.

At 41, Thomas Watson, Sr. was fired from National Cash Register. He went on to create IBM!

At 40, Henry Ford was just beginning to think about his Model T. Five years later, in 1900, he marketed that remarkably sturdy car for only $805!

At the age of 50, 11 years before taking over the presidency, Harry Truman failed as a farmer and businessman, a lame-duck country judge, and a minor pawn in the Kansas City, Missouri machine, according to *Newsweek*.

You know the rest of each of these stories. My point is simply this:

When you use your good brains—and borrow brains from others all around you—ANY AGE is the right age to make a contribution.

TO HELL with the "Peter Principle."

Now, let's get to work. Whatever we can do, we can do BETTER!

One of the most remarkable examples of the working of this creative power of mind was demonstrated by Albert Einstein. Working as a poor patent-office clerk in Berne, Switzerland, he had devoted every spare moment, night and day, for months, in an attempt to develop a mathematical formula by which he could prove the interrelationship of time, space and matter. Goaded by an unsympathetic wife, who urged him to give up his "fruitless quest" and spend all his time toward earning a better living, Einstein retired late one night, filled with a desperate now-or-never yearning.

Suddenly, in a deep dream state, a panoramic image of the universe illumined his Consciousness! He awakened with the knowledge he had been seeking: "The energy contained in any particle of matter is equal to the mass of that matter multiplied by the speed of light—one hundred and eighty-six thousand miles a second—and again multiplied by the speed of light."

All this, Einstein expressed in his now-famous formula: "E equals MC squared." Once possessed of this knowledge, it had taken Einstein three weeks to put it down on paper!

We can't always be Einsteins, but we all can make much more effective use of our powers of creativity. It all depends upon the kinds of images we place in Consciousness.

The story of the inventive genius Thomas A. Edison has often been told: how he had learned to call upon his creative power of mind; how he assembled all the facts he could determine about an object he wanted to invent, then turned all the experimental information over to his Subconscious and retired to a cot in his laboratory and let this imaginative faculty go to work on it. In due course of time, his Subconscious supplied him with the answers and ideas he sought. Edison recognized that his conscious mind contained no creative power in itself—that it was only a collector of the experience and the information needed for the creative power to produce the end result.

Many people who picture what they want, do it through prayer and address their needs to a Higher Power whom they often visualize as Jesus, if this has been their religious teaching. Whatever the concept—and I describe the Higher Power as "God the Great Intelligence"—there is no question but that there is a Power in our Subconscious that is not limited by Time or Space. This has been demonstrated in countless ways. Some folks refer to this Presence as a "guardian angel" who answers their calls for help, at times, and gives them guidance and protection far beyond their conscious knowing or ability.

James D. Sapp of Neptune Beach, Florida, has given me permission to reproduce his account of an answer he received through prayer, which he imaged to his concept of Jesus.

Several months ago, I was having extreme difficulty making my house payments and was far behind on them, which was causing me a great deal of concern. I had always believed in the power of prayer but, subconsciously at least, I considered it more as a supplement to my own efforts than a source of power in and of itself. However, as I was riding the bus home one afternoon, I began the usual practice of dozing off to sleep, which ordinarily came rather easy due to my working most every night on my second job.

I dreamed that I heard a voice saying, "When you go to God in prayer and whatever you ask, ask it in My Name and it shall be given to you." I thought, somehow, it was the voice of Jesus, and the dream seemed so real. So that evening, as soon as I had opportunity, I prayed for an improvement of my financial situation, if it was God's will, and particularly that I could make my house payments, and I prayed in the name of Jesus.

The following morning I received a telephone call from a friend whom I hadn't heard from in about two years and, following a few words of greeting, she said, "Jim, aren't you behind in your house payments?" Of course, I was stunned but admitted that I was. She said she had been burdened for me for the past several days since she arrived back in Jacksonville, but *especially since last night,* and felt that God had been leading her to me to help me in some way. She went on to say she had worked in Kansas and had been able to save some money and wanted to give me some to help with my house payments.

As first, I refused, for I knew how she had struggled before to make ends meet but she insisted, and said if I refused to let her help me, I would be preventing her from obeying God's command for she had a distinct feeling that He was directing her to help me.

We arranged a brief meeting on my lunch period that day when she drove me to my mortgage company and handed me the money for my house payment, which put me out of the "danger" zone. Although the episode took place several months ago, it continues to amaze me when I think of it, and I am convinced that all things are possible through prayer . . . and that prayer, and what you visualize through prayer, is a tremendous source of power.

I am reminded of the time you describe in one of your books of the *$1,000 which you needed very badly and received.*

I did have a similar experience, which may have value for you. In Mr. Sapp's case, his need was answered through a prayer addressed to Jesus. In my opinion, this same appeal directed to the God Power within, and not necessarily to Jesus, would have brought the same happening to pass.

People of all faiths throughout the world are getting answers to these forms of prayers and meditations, so it is obvious that these powers of mind are not the exclusive possession of any religion. They work even for those who profess to no faith in a deity but who picture vividly and earnestly what they want or need—and some power within them responds.

I have stated my conviction that a part of God, the Great Intelligence, dwells within each individual Consciousness and that this constitutes a possible communication network. Images of human needs can be transmitted and make contact, at times, with people, known and unknown to the sender, who are in position to be helpful to others.

Thus a form of telepathy takes place—as in the case of Mr. Sapp's friend, who "tuned in" and "sensed" his need, and felt impelled to go to his aid.

The similar incident in my life to which Mr. Sapp referred was reported by me in my book *How To Make ESP Work for You,* where the detailed account may be read. In brief, some years ago, I became stranded in Hollywood when a writing assignment fell through. I was not well known. I had no money, and I could think of no one to whom I could go for financial aid. Yet I needed $1,000 urgently, and I had to have it by noon of the following day. I could not ask for a loan at a bank, since as a freelance writer I had no regular income to back me up. So far as the business world was concerned, I was a poor risk. I was reduced to my final resource—I asked guidance from the Higher Power within.

The actual blueprint that I gave to my Subconscious mind envisioned its finding for me some person whom I might or might not know, but who, for one reason or another, would be willing to lend me $1,000. I placed no restriction upon where or through what association of circumstances or people this benefactor might be located.

My Creative Power was thus given a free hand. My only contribution was the removal of fears and doubts; and then, the exercise of faith in the ability of this Higher Power to bring me what I had pictured.

Once this was done, I dropped to sleep with the conviction that I would awaken in the morning and be guided as to what action to take in order to get the money.

When I awakened in the morning, my Conscious Mind instantly was alerted to receive the expected inner guidance, but no idea or sense of direction came to me. Instead, I felt that something had happened while I slept, and that all I had to do was to sit tight, remain relaxed, and await developments, not permitting any fear or worry to demagnetize the conditions that had been established.

This is always the most difficult kind of guidance to follow. It is much easier to feel that you can be doing something to help produce what is desired. You are impressed by the passage of time and the feeling that time will run out before what you need is realized. This is the point at which many people become panicky and desperate and cut themselves off from contact with their inner minds in a last-minute attempt to force a result.

Around 10:30 in the morning, the phone rang. It was Wesley Barr, managing editor of the *Los Angeles Herald-Express,* a man I had only met recently when he had interviewed me concerning my experiments in long-distance telepathy with Sir Hubert Wilkins. During the course of the conversation, he asked me out of a clear sky, "Sherman, is there anything I can do for you?"

"Yes," I said, on impulse, as my inner voice instructed. "I need a thousand dollars. Can you help me get it?"

"I'll call you back in ten minutes," he said. In five minutes, Barr was back on the phone. "You are to have lunch in downtown Los Angeles at the Jonathan Club with Eugene Overton, a friend of mine," he said. "Tell him what you need and why you need it. It's all fixed."

I kept my appointment and met a most unusual man, one of the best-known and best-liked attorneys on the West Coast. This man handed me—someone he had never seen before—a check for $1,000, simply on the word of Wesley Barr, who scarcely knew me himself!

Here again is evidence that when we, as individuals, give expression to a deep desire for the solution of a serious problem, or the achievement of a difficult objective, our minds, through the channel of Cosmic Consciousness, are brought in contact with the minds of others, consciously known or unknown to us, who have like interests and who therefore are prepared to respond to our call.

It must be clearly understood that this function of mind is not a form of so-called black magic or hypnotic influence. When alignments are made between individuals by action of these higher powers of mind, no element of force enters in. These people are not compelled to be of service. They are only given the opportunity to make a free-will choice to help us, once they are brought in touch and acquainted with our situation.

Since like always attracts like in the realm of mind, you can look back over your life with the functioning of this law in mind and easily see the part that positive and negative thinking has played in the things, good and bad, that have happened.

A perfect example of the working of this law in *reverse* was recently reported to me by Mrs. D. S. of Conrad, Montana. She told me that everything she pictured for herself and family turned out just the opposite. Then she cited example after example to prove her point, stating that she had read my book, *How to Foresee and Control Your Future* and had found it to be a good book but felt that it just didn't apply to everybody.

> Despite all my visualizing, I have had some very opposite things happen to me. The Conscious and Subconscious fight against me all the time. It is about to drive me crazy. I have to think backward all the while and by that, I mean just that. In order to have something good happen, I have to think the worst! Here is an example:
>
> I always said and thought I could and would not live in a trailer house—and guess where I am living today (in a trailer!) I only wanted two children. I have *four!*

My sister's oldest girl rocked so hard in a chair, it would come down with a bang. I thought I couldn't stand it—but guess what—all four of my children did this . . . if I think things over and decide on something, it always comes out backwards.

Here are some other examples: I was driving uptown one day and it crossed my mind that I hadn't had any wrecks and no tickets since I had been driving. Guess what—that very afternoon a train hit me! . . . One day, my husband, kids and I were driving up to Moose Lake, Minnesota from Hastings. Just out of town there was a car broke down and I *thought* I would sure hate to be broke down out here. I'm so glad our car is in good shape. Well, we got 17 miles up the road, and our car *quit!*

If I get up in a good mood in the morning, and think, "Gee, I feel good"—before long something happens to ruin my day. . . . If I think I should lose weight and make up my mind to do so, I catch myself eating more.

I wanted and prayed for my oldest girl to be able to get a job and make it on her own, and this is a very deep feeling and is with me all the time, but she has been out on her own for six months and still doesn't have a steady job, and can't make it on her own.

I could go on and on—but I am sure you can see what I mean by *backwards.* I have to think negative to get positive results. Can you explain this to me?

My answer: It is possible, in the case of Mrs. D. S., that she is able to sense, at times, events coming toward her in time. This is called precognition. Once she senses such a possible happening, she then may try to picture just the opposite; but the causative forces are too strong to circumvent, and her premonition comes true, in whole or in part.

However, in MOST of the examples cited, her fears and worries caused her to CREATE or ATTRACT the very things she did not want to occur.

You can want something with your Conscious Mind; but if your Subconscious is more deeply impressed with the feeling you won't get it, the opposite, as Mrs. D. S.

has testified, is apt to happen. For this reason, it is wise to analyze your feelings to make sure that your fears or apprehensions are not counteracting the good things you are trying to visualize for your future.

Here is a case of a seven-year-old girl who let nothing spoil her image of what she wanted. She held to her picture with all her mind and heart despite everything that seemed to indicate it wouldn't come true. The story is told by Kim's mother, Mrs. Connie Halterman of San Diego, California:

My husband and I have four children: Kathy, Karen, Kim, and Kirk. Kathy's bicycle was passed down to Karen when Karen was old enough to ride it, and Kathy received a larger bicycle. When Kim was old enough to handle a two-wheeler, she and Karen "shared" the second bike. A boy's bike was then passed on to us by a nephew—and because Kirk was the only boy, it naturally became his. (He handled it proficiently at four years of age.) And so it was that Kim was the only child who didn't have a bike of her "very own."

How she longed for a bike!! We promised her that we would buy her one as soon as we could manage, but it would probably take quite a while to gather that much spare money. A bicycle just was *not* in the budget.

Kim was not discouraged by this news. She continued to wish for a bicycle and often talked about the bicycle she would get very soon.

Ten days before her birthday she made a wish on a rabbit's foot and told us that her wish would come true. *She would get a bike on her seventh birthday!* The fact that the money for a bike still was not in the budget was of no concern to her. Her optimism could not be shaken, no matter how hard we tried to explain that we couldn't possibly get a bike in time for her birthday.

That same week, Kim's grandfather (my father) WON a bicycle in a contest. With seven grandchildren and only one bike, he wasn't quite sure about what he should do with it. Then he learned that Kim was the only grandchild without a bike to call her own. Plans were set in motion to have the bike delivered on her birthday.

On the afternoon of her seventh birthday, a truck arrived in front of our house. Kim was in the backyard. We called to her in the back, "Kim, someone is here to see you!"

She RAN into the house, screaming for joy: *"My bike is here! My bike is here!"*

And when she got to the front porch, there it was . . . a shiny, beautiful hot-pink bicycle of her very own!!

Her strong desire surely must have worked to her advantage!

It unquestionably DID work to Kim's advantage. A positive mental attitude toward life—whatever happens to you—will always stimulate the CREATIVE POWER WITHIN to help produce as well as attract to you whatever you VISUALIZE!

CHAPTER 13

The Power of Imagery on Film

Astounding proof that we think basically in pictures has been produced by the spontaneous projection on film—especially Polaroid—of faces, forms, and well-known places and scenes by such sensitives as Ted Serios, Willi Schwanholz, three members of one family—Joseph, Richard, and Fred Vielleux in Waterville, Maine—and a fourteen-year-old Japanese boy, Masuaki Kiyota. These people are among the most prominent sensitives today who possess this unusual psychic ability, but there is a long-recorded history of people who have discovered images on photographs they have taken, which have contained faces of friends and loved ones who have left this life. Their findings would indicate that the "mental ether" is filled with images of all sorts, past as well as present, and that countless mental pictures are being broadcast by the minds of all people, at all times, which can occasionally be captured by the eye of a camera, held in the hands of a person who possesses a special psychic power.

There is speculation that these energized images somehow emanate from the minds of living as well as deceased persons, dependent on the conditions existing at the moment, and impress themselves upon sensitized film.

A scientist who has made an extensive study of people possessing this paranormal photographic ability is Professor Walter Uphoff of Oregon, Wisconsin, who has observed the work of many sensitives. He is on the research staff of our ESP Research Associates Foundation, and he has traveled the world in his investigation of various forms of psychic phenomena. He and his wife Mary Jo are a research team and are authors of a comprehensive book, *New Psychic Frontiers,* in which this subject is covered.

In recounting the highlights of his research on the ability of some minds to transmit images onto film, Walter said:

More and more investigators of the psychic are beginning to realize the tremendous, but largely unused potential of the human mind. To what extent this energy functions with or without help from "other dimensions" will be debated for some time.

One of the most unusual persons to appear on the psychic scene in recent times is Willi Schwanholz. Things which happen in his presence are baffling, but also may provide some clues or insights into the dynamics involved when an individual learns to concentrate and can direct or focus his mental energy (like a laser beam?) rather than letting it disperse in all directions.

Although Schwanholz has produced many paranormal photographs on Polaroid film and has obtained voices on tapes, some of the pictures he has projected defy explanation. A photographic expert who has examined some of the pictures has opined: "Anyone who could produce that effect by natural means would have a job with a television network." But Schwanholz has no elaborate equipment and knows nothing about electronic synthesizers.

Schwanholz, born in Germany about forty-eight years ago, still has a pronounced German accent, and when excited about his strange pictures, pours forth a rapid-fire monologue which can be somewhat difficult to understand. Coming from a family of circus performers, he appeared in Canada in high-wire acts which included riding a motorcycle on a cable. After migrating to Chicago, he returned on a visit to Germany in the fall of 1975, and was astonished to find his face had appeared on a Super-8 movie which had been made by friends in Frankfurt—*while Willi was still in Chicago!* In discussing this event, Willi recalled that he had been sick at the time the movie was made and had slept straight through twenty-five hours! This raised a question in my mind: had Willi taken an "astral trip" to visit old friends during his sleep—and had they somehow captured his image on their film?

Puzzled by this inexplicable happening, Willi sought out Ted Serios, who had projected hundreds of images onto Polaroid film, in seeking an answer to this phenomenon. Ted handed him a Polaroid camera and asked him to see if he could demonstrate by starting shooting and pointing the camera in the direction of his head. The second shot Willi made showed a shadowy church dome which resembled one with which he was familiar in Frankfurt. On his seventh attempt, the image of a bikini-clad girl appeared on the film, the first of a series of such recurring "visitors." In one instance, after he had gotten a picture of one of the scantily attired girls, he addressed the camera: "Come as God made you," and sure enough, on his next try, he got a picture of this feminine figure *sans bikini!*

One of the photos Willi produced in the presence of Curtis and Mary Fuller (publisher and editor of FATE Magazine respectively) along with Ted Serios, was an unusual pattern which, at first glance, looked like a snakeskin. On closer examination, about a dozen faces in a series could be seen in the portion of the picture which was *in focus*. At both ends, the "snakeskin" was less distinct and it happened that the images might have been superimposed on each other.

Some of the faces were repeated at least eight to a dozen times across the top of the photograph—one of them resembled a baseball player. Quite a number of faces seemed to overlap each other. The only explanation which occurred to me for the multiple effect is that the mind may have been sending a series of impulses in rapid succession because I observed that Willi's head appeared to "vibrate" when he was sufficiently "revved up" to produce a photograph.

It became apparent that Willi ordinarily had no conscious control of the type of picture which might be projected from his mental storehouse of images. But it also seemed clear that Willi had physically seen most of these scenes or peoples at some time in his actual life, and was calling them forth at random during his concentrations. Most certainly, they were not figments of his imagination. They were images that had been recorded in some previous moment in his consciousness.

One evening, Willie was using Ted Serios's mother's Polaroid camera with a flash and produced the picture of a face which looked familiar, but he had no idea whose it was. Several other attempts revealed unusual energy patterns but nothing recognizable. Later, when Willi stopped at the First Distributor Store on Pulaski near West Laurence, where he purchased film, he showed the unusual picture to the manager, Andy Bury, who exclaimed, "Why, that's Carl Grayson, WGN's late-news sportscaster!"

When I heard this incredible story, I decided to do some sleuthing. A call to Channel 9 confirmed that they did indeed have a Carl Grayson on the staff. When Hilton Hanna, a Chicago friend, visited in January, he assured me that the photograph did resemble Grayson, whom he had seen on TV many times. The next step was to ask Grayson for an interview and, in February 1977, I went to WGN-TV, Chicago, and waited in the lunchroom until Mr. Grayson was free to see me. A fellow WGN announcer, who was having a snack, to whom we showed the photograph, said, "Yes, it does look like him!"

About 7:10 P.M. in walked a tall, graying man, wearing dark shirt, no tie, who did resemble the multiple image in Willi's picture. Did he, when on camera, wear a white or light shirt, dark jacket, dark tie? "Yes," he said. "Why do you ask?" He looked at the photo we handed to him and exclaimed in astonishment: *"My gosh—that's what I look like on the monitor!"*

Now, how could this possibly have come about? Skeptics, whether they have a technical background in photography or not, usually say, "That's a fake, or trick photo," without troubling to ask any questions about the circumstances or the processes purportedly producing such a picture of a recognizable face. Anyone seeking facts must try to think of all possible explanations for any phenomena encountered. Therefore, one must speculate as to how Willi might possibly have faked the picture.

He was in our home with Serios on March 6 and 7, in 1976, where we witnessed his obtaining less clear but definitely paranormal Polaroid pictures. It was obvious to us that producing the effect would require extensive equipment. A great number of photographs would have to have been obtained from individuals or public sources, as well as the expenditure of an enormous amount of time to prepare the montage or mock-up, necessary for the photographing of such a picture—if indeed this could even be done successfully.

Willi produced these paranormals, under our observation, without any special equipment—merely by holding the camera between his knees, breathing deeply and vibrating his head vigorously as he tripped the shutter. There was no reason for our doubting his account of how the photographs were produced. Even so, we checked his work with a number of photographic experts, all of whom said it would be very difficult and extremely expensive, if not impossible, to simulate such pictures.

This led to the conclusion that Ted Serios, Willi, and others somehow possess the psychic ability to mentally project images onto film. With respect to the image Willi produced of the TV news commentator, Carl Grayson, we assume that his eyes must have seen Grayson on the TV screen at some time, when his brain recorded the image and his subconscious somehow selected it to project on the film. Why this image of Grayson should have appeared, which had no meaning to Willi, is another one of the mysteries.

One thing I learned in my years of parapsychological investigation is that whatever hypothesis one comes up with to explain a certain phenomenon, it is likely to be inadequate to cover the entire field. In Willi's case, how does one explain, for example, the pictures of girls whom Willi does not know and cannot recall having seen—or other pictures such as an old man in shirt sleeves . . . or an Asian goddess . . . or other images which Willi feels may represent scenes from outer space?

In Tokyo, Japan, last October, I became acquainted with a fourteen-year-old schoolboy, Masuaki Kiyota, and his family. I witnessed Masuaki project an image of the Keio Plaza Hotel where I was staying, on Polaroid film, at his home about ten miles from the hotel. In a second try, he got the upper half of the same hotel with the TV antennas on top. (The Japanese call this kind of phenomenon "Nengraphy.")

A question that might be asked—did Masuaki receive the image of the hotel from my mind by telepathy and then project it subconsciously on the film? So often these "projectors" cannot predict in advance what images will appear. It is remarkable enough whatever theory is deduced to explain the phenomenon.

Take the case of the remarkably psychically gifted Joseph Veilleux and his two sons, Fred and Richard, of Waterville, Maine. For some years now, they have been receiving hundreds of images of faces and forms of people who have left this life! When I first visited them on May 17–18, 1969, having with me a Polaroid camera and fresh films, I learned that they had stumbled onto this picture-taking process "on instructions from a Ouija board."

They showed me scores of pictures, some of which had been taken at particular times and places, following Ouija board directions. The Veilleuxs make their living as building and construction trade workers and have played with the Ouija board out of curiosity. Quite often the distinct faces of deceased people appear surrounded by a white cloudlike effect. There may be as many as a cluster of faces, transparently appearing over the actual physical landscape at which the camera has been aimed . . . or superimposed upon the forms of living persons.

Here is a different type of phenomenon because it is obvious that these images are not coming from the minds of the picture-takers. They are being transmitted from some outside source, perhaps drawing upon the psychic energy of the person doing the photographing, but otherwise completely apart from anything of his doing.

Are we to accept, as a fact, that spirit entities, in the very atmosphere about us, are able to manifest their presence by projecting recognizable images of their former likeness on earth, utilizing still-unknown psychic energies?

As Walter Uphoff related these evidential cases of psychic photography that he had personally explored, I was reminded of a baffling case that had been reported to me by Alfred Cheney Johnston, the official photographer of Florenz Ziegfeld's beautiful showgirls. This experience dated back to the 1920s when I was then living in New York. I have told about it in detail in my book *Your Power to Heal*, but it deserves retelling here as a graphic illustration of the ability of the minds of those, living and "dead," to project images.

In those days I had written plays for Broadway and knew quite a number of show people, among them Mr. Johnston. One day he invited me to come to his studio, saying that he had a picture of a Ziegfeld beauty he wanted me to see.

"What I am going to show you," he said, as he took a photographic plate and print from his voluminous files, "is something that I will never let out of my hands. If I did, I think you'll agree, the release of this photo might cost me my reputation. A skeptical, scoffing public would accuse me of trying to perpetrate a hoax. The reason I am taking you into my confidence is because I want your opinion as a psychic."

With this, Johnston gave me the 8 × 10 photograph to gaze upon, continuing to describe it as I looked in open amazement.

"When I developed this shot myself from a dozen different poses of this Follies beauty, I couldn't believe my eyes. These spirit faces—seven of them, as you see, all clear and unmistakable—surrounded the star on only this one of the twelve negatives. The other eleven plates came out in what might be called 'normal shape.' But something obviously happened when this shot was taken, something that will leave me wondering the rest of my days."

My first question to Johnston: "What did the star think of the picture? Did you show it to her?"

"Indeed I did," said Johnston, "first making her promise to say nothing to anyone. What shocked me even more was that she instantly recognized five of the seven faces as those of deceased relatives! Only two could not be identified. I am assuming that they were dead friends of her loved ones or other relatives she had never seen or known. I get goose pimples now as I tell you this. I had always made fun of psychic phenomena, ghosts and the like."

"Did you ask the star if she herself was psychic? She might have had mediumistic ability, powers which had attracted these spirit entities to her?"

"No, this was as great a surprise to her as it had been to me," said Johnston. "There's just no human way to account for this. I've taken over 25,000 pictures of beauties in my day and nothing like this has happened before. As far as I'm concerned, I'm ready for it never to happen again!"

I examined the photograph carefully. It was against a dark background that the lighter spirit faces appeared. There was a slight luminous quality about them. Johnston went on to say that the star had brought in photographs of some of the relatives and that they had matched up. Could these have been thought images from the mind of the star? Were they stored in her Subconscious? She may never have seen the two she did not recognize, and thus she would have no mental imprint of them. The fact that the two images of the seven were not identifiable tends to disprove the theory of thought projection. Why should they have appeared at all if they had been coming from her Consciousness? Certainly she was not consciously thinking of them.

Fifty years ago, Dr. Tomokichi Fukurai, a Japanese psychical researcher, experimented with mediums whom he found could project and imprint mental images on photographic plates. He called this phenomenon "Thoughtography."

Today, there are literally thousands of authenticated psychic photographs in existence. They have been produced under test conditions in many countries of the world and by many methods. They have been produced in the light, in the dark, on regular and infrared films, by holding plates or films between hands, or by wearing them on the person, by projecting mental impressions onto the emulsion, and in other ways, none of which have been satisfactorily explained by scientific investigation.

It is the opinion of Olga Worrell, world-renowned spiritual healer, herself a psychic medium, that one of the main purposes of psychic photography appears to be the proving of a continued existence after death. "Even so," warns Olga, "allowing for the fact that genuine psychic photography does occur, it can also be faked, and often is—so we should not allow ourselves to be deceived."

CHAPTER 14

One Man's Use of Imagery

From 6:30 to 7:30 every Thursday morning, when he is in the States, John Robinson, one of the world's best-known international shipping specialists, keeps an appointment in his home town of Tiburon, California, with his psychiatrist, Dr. Gerald Jampolsky. He sees him at this odd time so that it will not interfere with his working day, as he is undoubtedly one of the busiest and most dynamic individuals anyone can ever meet. These appointments mean a great deal to Robinson because Dr. Jampolsky has taught him a visualizing process which he says is largely responsible for his spectacular success in life. Of course, Robinson had been given a running start by studying and applying Dr. Norman Vincent Peale's *The Power of Positive Thinking* and Dale Carnegie's *How to Win Friends and Influence People,* following up with the Dale Carnegie courses in public speaking, business management, and similar philosophies which he has since

161

passed on to many of his 1,400 employees. But Robinson's use of the higher powers of the mind—of picturing what he wanted to accomplish in life—took full flower in the past fifteen years with the inspirational and instructional help of psychiatrist Jampolsky. Today, a robust fifty-four years of age, Robinson exudes a contagious enthusiasm and self-confidence as he tells what positive picturing has done and is doing for him.

John Robinson heads the Harper Group, a conglomerate of shipping companies, which has ninety-six branches on six continents of the world. This group is rated first in international freight forwarding worldwide, and third in international freight forwarding in the United States.

This extensive enterprise keeps John Robinson in the air most of the time, traveling back and forth across the United States four months each year in this country, and five or six months jetting around the world. He started his business trips with a trip to Japan in the 1960s and has since made over 150 trips to Japan and the Orient, an unbelievable travel record.

The only way I could manage an interview with him was to tell him what I wanted him to tell me about himself on the phone, and then catching him aloft on American Airlines Flight 14, on January 8, 1978, enroute from San Francisco to New York, talking into a tape recorder, while he imagined that I was sitting beside him, for stimulation.

John Robinson now lives with images and imaginings. This practice of visualization is with him every waking moment. He takes whoever he is thinking about along with him wherever he goes—and communicates with that person as though he or she is physically present. He believes "one hundred percent," as he says, that he *is* or *can* be in touch on subconscious levels with members of his family, business associates, new people he is destined to meet—and that the way he thinks about others can bring a similar response from them.

This, to John Robinson, is living whole-istically—to use a phrase—calling, as nearly as possible, upon the total potential of his powers of mind, projecting pictures of what he plans to accomplish, including others in the picture who are associated or are to be associated, in his visualizations.

In John Robinson's visits to the various branches of his company throughout the world, he makes it a point to talk personally to his truckers, his warehouse people, clerks and employees in every department—not just executives—telling them how much he loves them and appreciates the work they are doing—that work for them should be fun. If it isn't fun, perhaps they should be working for someone else. He has learned that people can make things happen the way they want instead of letting things happen which they don't want—if they can just eliminate any angers or fears or worries, difficult as this may be at the start—in order to change what needs to be changed in their lives.

It is all a matter of right picturing and imaging. John Robinson says he has perfected this "thought system" which he has always used in part, in the past four years of his consultations with Dr. Jampolsky who has convinced him of the importance of "seeing where you are going before you get there" and then "filling in the pieces of what you need to visualize" when you arrive, so you maintain control of your mind at all times. To do this, says Robinson, is "to be creating a road map of your life," so that you can remove the tensions and fears from your Consciousness, no matter what the economic conditions around you or what others are doing or thinking of a negative nature.

Robinson tells of a time when he left Peoria with an associate on Ozark Airlines, forty-five minutes behind schedule, with the need to make a close connection out of Chicago on United. His associate expressed concern they would not make it. "Oh, yes, we will," assured Robinson, "if we just picture this plane making up time and if we picture our United flight not taking off till we get there." When they arrived, they grabbed their traveling bags and started running. The associate felt it was no use, that it was already time for the United flight departure. "Keep going!" insisted Robinson. "I feel we'll still make it." When they arrived at the gate, the steps had been withdrawn and the United plane was starting to pull out. Appealing to the agent, Robinson cried, "We're supposed to be on that flight. Call the captain, please, and have him let down the steps." The agent grabbed the phone and made contact with the pilot. The plane stopped, the door opened, the steps came down, and Robinson and his associate dashed out and boarded.

"I accept whatever happens as a miracle," says Robinson, "and I don't try to explain it. I thank God, of course, and whatever powers there be, many times a day, because I feel I am getting help in accordance with the way I am visualizing. If things don't quite work out, on occasion, I don't get upset. I hold the thought that something good or better will grow out of it. It is easy to let your mind put you on the wrong track and start picturing the worst happening. You have to be on guard against this. It's a part of the old thought pattern of letting fear and worry and anger and tension rule your life.

"Some years ago," confessed Robinson, "since I had not gone to church since I was a boy—I decided it would be a good thing for my family—my wife and daughter and son—to have a church affiliation, so they joined St. John's Episcopal Church. (My daughter is now a freshman at Colorado University, and my son attends a high school in our suburban community.)

"It wasn't long, however, before my wife and children impressed upon me that what I thought would be good for them, would also be good for me—so I joined, too. My tendency, when I go into anything, is to go all the way. I became a vestryman and haven't missed a Sunday in the last four years, when I have been home.

"As I reentered religious life, I prayed hard that I might become an outstanding leader in my field, and that I would make big profits—a lot of money. I wanted to be something my father had never been able to achieve. He had attained only a sixth-grade education, but he had formed a small freight forwarding company in 1898, and operated one branch in San Francisco with eleven employees. I went through the University of California in two and a half years, then spent three and a half years in the navy as a lieutenant in the Pacific area, where there was plenty of shooting. I came out after the war, reentered the University of California and graduated from the business school—then joined my father's company, learned the business, became a leader in the local shipping community, and, in time, was recognized as a specialist in international air freight, customs brokerage, and international freight forwarding. With this as a background, I had begun to picture expansion—and the business has grown to the immense proportions it enjoys today. In 1977, after having been a private corporation for seventy-seven years, we have gone public, so that outsiders could buy stock and participate in the profits with us—something that was predicted couldn't be done since we had to declare our inside operations, financial condition, and secure permission from government agencies, a seemingly hopeless bureaucratic achievement.

"But holding the right picture, despite all manner of setbacks, making public disclosures of everything we had done, requiring the expenditure of $100,000 in legal fees alone, I announced that we would be able to make a public offering on June twenty-first, 1977! People in the know said it was a million-to-one chance against putting this change through, but I arranged a victory dinner for the night of June twenty-first. My ten attorneys said I was crazy, but I had had too many demonstrations of the power of mind to be dissuaded.

"Well, I missed it by ONE day. We held the celebration at Trader Vic's on the night of the twenty-first of June . . . and the grant for the public offering came to us on June *twenty-second!*

"Looking back over the several years it took us to make this change, I recalled the tests of faith I had undergone. I had declared my own holdings of more than two million and thereupon sold a sizable block of my shares at $13.00 a share. As I had grown in understanding, I had become more and more aware of the needs of others and the desire to be helpful to them, that money wasn't everything, that while it was fine to use the power of visualization to bring money and business success, it was more worthwhile and satisfying to use my resources, material and spiritual, to aid all within my reach, who were deserving of assistance, to share what knowledge I had of the power of mind, the same power that every person, white or black, possessed, and could learn to use for his own benefit and advancement."

Robinson said that he had felt the influence of his mother, who had always been interested in diet and exercise. She believed that health depended largely on not only what you took into your mind but what you took into your mouth—and that exercise was equally important.

With these thoughts in mind, Robinson decided he should be taking more care of his body, so he set up a schedule of running three to four miles each morning, five days a week, and from six to ten miles each Saturday and Sunday, a practice he is continuing today.

But Robinson, as he runs, is not only exercising his body, he is exercising his mind. He tells me he is picturing what he hopes to achieve in business that day, his plans for the future, and is sending out helpful thoughts to others whom he senses need better physical and mental health.

Says Robinson: "I discovered that I could get greater guidance in this manner than I could in church. I wasn't just listening to ministers and others—I was doing something *for* and *in* myself . . . activating these Higher Powers to go to work for me—to put magnetic forces in motion to attract what I pictured to me—and to stimulate the functioning of these same powers in the minds of loved ones and friends."

A technique of visualizing which Robinson worked out, while running, was as unique as it was effective. It occurred to him, being very time conscious, having studied time management, that he might profit doubly by exercising his mind at the same time he was exercising his body.

After all, mind was a tool, created to be used, and what provided a better opportunity than giving his Conscious Mind's attention to the passing scenery as he ran while seeing scenes in his mind's eye of real-life objectives he was working on? I've heard inventors testify they had gotten some of their best ideas while shaving or under a shower, and women claim they got their best results from praying while washing dishes! Why shouldn't Robinson have similar success while jogging? He told me he had run miles and miles picturing over and over again the conversion of his company from private to public ownership.

"As I became more and more aware of the creative power of thought, not only in my own life, but as applied to the health and emotional and business problems of others, I began to experimentally direct my thought images in an attempt to help them. One day a deeply depressed personal friend of mine told me he was in bad physical shape and was slated for surgery. I said to him, "Don't you let them operate. Call it off. Come to San Francisco and see me. Take my medicine. Start running with me. Get your circulation going. Then go to Hong Kong and let them treat you with acupuncture. Let go of your tensions and fears." He said he'd think it over.

"The next morning, I took my friend with me in my imagination. I spoke to him as though he was actually present. I said, 'Hello, Fred. We're going to start off nice and easy so you can keep pace with me. Now, you just let my body be your body . . . I'm going to let myself feel as you feel. I'm taking on all those fears and tensions and anger and depression you've been carrying around with you . . . and as we pass this garbage can, I'm going to take them and dump them all in . . . and I can feel all these disturbances disappearing from your body . . . and I'm fastening a balloon to this can, and there it goes, can and all, into the sky . . . taking all your fears and tensions and anger and depression away from you. . . . They're all gone . . . and your body isn't weighted down any more . . . you feel like your old, good self again . . . you're not going to need an operation. You're a well man!"

Every morning thereafter, as Robinson ran, he repeated this visualization, taking Fred and his body along with him in his imagination. Finally he heard from his friend, who told him, "I don't know what is happening . . . but

I'm feeling better. I think I had better come to see you."
The friend came to San Francisco and listened in wonder
as Robinson told him what he had been doing. He was so
impressed that he made the trip to Hong Kong, as Robinson had suggested, took the acupuncture treatments, and
now, after two years, is enjoying fine health.

Since then, Robinson has used refinements of this im-
agery-transmission method, creating thought pictures
which apparently have reached the minds of afflicted persons and provided the imagery that they have needed
for the healing power within them to bring about the desired or needed change in body chemistry.

Robinson's wife Patsy was threatened with glaucoma.
Her mother had suffered from it, said it had run in the
family, and that her daughter would probably get it as she
got older. This suggestion had been enough to cause this
tendency to develop. Once again, Robinson took Patsy
with him on his runs, talked to her, visualized a group of
snakes—a cobra, a boa constrictor, a rattlesnake, a water
snake, and other forms of snakes—threatening her eyesight. Then he put them all in a basket, fastening them to
a balloon and cast the balloon adrift, carrying them away
from Patsy so they could menace her no more. He repeated this visualization—and each day the snakes got
smaller and less menacing in size, until they disappeared
altogether, and the threat of glaucoma diminished in pro-
portion.

"You can create your own pictures of whatever you
wish to rid yourself," directed Robinson. "It sounds fantastic, I know, but it works! The creative power of mind
has to have something to work on. It doesn't reason—
it just takes what you give it and uses it as a blueprint to
produce the results you want. The snakes, for example,
were just symbolic of Patsy's threatened eye trouble. The
healing energies went to work to correct the eye condition, and the snakes I pictured, symbolic of the trouble,
had to disappear along with the disappearance of the
glaucoma.

"Whatever you imagine, you must believe—*one hundred percent!* You must develop super self-confidence.

Never ask why these seeming miracles happen. Just expect them—and accept them! And thank God, the Higher Power within you, for them!"

Our company image is designed to encourage and inspire our employees to LIVE IN THE NOW!

We have the figure of a man named MR. NOW!

MR. NOW is standing on a box, between two big rocks. The Rock on the left as you are looking at him contains one word: YESTERDAY. The Rock on his right, the word: TOMORROW.

Yesterday is gone—Tomorrow never comes—

The Only Time there is—IS NOW!

Printed on the box, underneath the figure of MR. NOW are the words:

> SELF-CONFIDENCE
> AWARENESS
> LOVE
> HAPPINESS

TODAY IS THE BEST DAY OF MY LIFE!
IT IS THE ONLY DAY OF MY LIFE!
MY OPPORTUNITY FOR REAL HAPPINESS IS RIGHT NOW!

CHAPTER 15

How to Get Rid of Wrong Images

Quite a number of convicts who write me from different penitentiaries have read books of mine, especially *How to Take Yourself Apart and Put Yourself Together Again.* Here are some consolidated excerpts from men who are serving life sentences for murder, robbery, and rape.

Dear Mr. Sherman:

I wish there was some way that everyone could read your book. It is just what we all need to learn to live and think right. . . . It would mean much more to us than vocational training. . . . The prison authorities are doing nothing to help us improve our minds or mental attitudes. . . . I cannot guarantee that if they let me out and I get hungry and desperate enough that I won't kill again. . . . One of the victims attacked me and it was either me or him. I haven't been able to make myself feel sorry for what I did. That's why I say that vocational training is not the basic answer. In my opinion, training of the mind is the only hope of rehabilitation. I've got to find some way to get rid of the images of hate and resentment and rejection I've been carrying around in my mind. If I can't, I know I can't trust myself out in so-called decent society. Your book is opening up new doors to me. I've let some of my fellow inmates read it. We've had bull sessions on it. That's why I say thoughts like you have expressed can do more to change the attitudes of the criminally minded than anything else. We all need insight on ourselves, as to the mental and emotional causes of our misconduct. There are not enough psychiatrists to go around . . . and they don't have the time or any personalized method for reaching the mind of the individual. The way things are now, the criminal population is going to keep on increasing and most of us won't be any better or different when we get out, if we do, than we are now.

These comments are representative of the many letters I have received and am receiving from people, in jail or out, who are having mental and emotional problems and are seeking a solution. Some are on the verge of suicide; others have resorted to the use of a gun to settle their disagreements and disputes; still others are struggling to meet situations which they find beyond their power to cope.

It is evident that the widespread possession of firearms has contributed to the temptation of many people to deal with their problems through violence. There is little education in a gun except how to kill and how to rule by force. These are the two primitive, protective urges of man. Negotiating with words instead of bullets is risking annihilation. The surest way to ensure survival is to liquidate anyone who opposes you. Today, with all the facade of civilization, the law of the jungle still prevails. Millions of young men in all countries are trained with weapons of destruction. Their lower natures are stimulated by the images of killing to the point that their higher, finer impulses are dwarfed and undeveloped.

The savage teaching of "kill or be killed" is so innate that the instinct to kill as a means of getting one's own way or eliminating any opposition is carried over into civilian life. We have bred and are breeding a generation of emotionally unstable potential murderers, with little respect for life, property, or the law of the land.

Think of the minds today that are filled with destructive images—hates and prejudices that have been passed down by parents to children and on to their children, in an endless stream of ill feeling toward others and disturbed feelings toward themselves. How is this self-perpetuating condition ever to be alleviated? How can mankind ever learn what it is doing to itself by the constant harboring of such devastating inhuman images? Why can't people realize that nothing can happen, anytime, anywhere, until and unless it has first been pictured by some mind or minds? Why shouldn't it be obvious that if enough minds project images of hate and distrust toward others, the ultimate consequences can only produce violence and destruction?

Hitler projected images of the Master Race into the minds of millions of Germans until the images possessed them, inflamed their minds with racial hatred and the urge for conquest, and brought on the Second World War. This can and will happen again unless human beings everywhere can be moved to change their thinking. Is this too much to hope?

You've heard all this before—that any change begins with *you*. Since feelings generate the power behind thought, you need to take inventory of your present feelings toward others—your friends and loved ones, your neighbors, business associates, everyone. Wrapped up in all these feelings is your total outlook on life. If you find certain feelings in certain areas are not what they should be, you can be sure they are affecting your body chemistry to the point of possible ill health as well as a potentially harmful mental attitude.

What is a bad image? It is any image which tends to hurt yourself or others. How can you get rid of it? There is one effective way. It is through using the power of meditation—by focusing your thoughts on your Inner Self and trying to see yourself as you really are, as others may have seen you. You may find there has been much in your life for which you will have to forgive yourself and others, or you will carry the scars of these unhappy and injurious experiences as long as you live—and they will continue to affect the health of your body and mind.

You may have sought to bury the memory images of tragic past episodes, but they have come to the surface at different times and caused you to renew your feelings of grief as well as possible hate and resentment. If so, the time has arrived for you to put an end to these cancerous sores which you have been carrying around in your Consciousness.

It is not easy to look back upon some of these now-regrettable experiences, but the rewards of facing them and making an adjustment toward them, are incalculable.

For many years, our ESP Research Associates Foundation has presented an Annual Body, Mind, and Spirit Healing Workshop, at which people from every state and an increasing number of foreign countries participate with me in a series of self-developing meditations.

I prepare the Workshoppers for each meditation by telling them that I will pause long enough after each statement to give them opportunity to repeat it mentally in their own minds and thus make it a part of their consciousness. When I use the word "I," and they repeat the statement, the "I" is to apply to them. Each meditation is addressed to each person's concept of God or the Higher Power within.

Now I invite you to take part in what possibly will be a new and personalized meditative exercise—one that I call "The Prayer of Forgiveness," which was among those presented at our recent Workshop.

As you read the printed words, VISUALIZE my speaking these statements—then *reread* each statement and apply it to yourself. Let the full meaning and feeling take hold of you. Let your thoughts go back in time to unhappy experiences in your life which you would like to remove. Call upon the Higher Power within to give you the strength of mind and spirit to correct mistakes you have made—as you resolve to forget and forgive.

This is YOUR MEDITATIVE MOMENT:

I am giving thought to the times when I have permitted myself to engage in thoughts of hate and bitterness and resentment . . .

For injuries which I feel I have suffered at the hands of loved ones and friends and acquaintances . . .

Whom I have trusted . . . and who may have mistreated or misguided or taken advantage of me . . . in my business and personal life . . .

I confess, Dear Father . . . that I have been unable to forgive and forget . . .

What I have felt to be grievous injustices done to me . . .

Instead, I have hoped to get even or seek revenge in some form . . . and have wished ill of that person or persons . . .

I now realize in retrospect, that I have often been so mentally and emotionally upset . . .

That I have not been able to see myself in perspective . . . nor willing to bear my possible share of the responsibility for what has happened . . .

Help me to remember that there are two sides to every situation . . .

I now concede that I may have been partially if not wholly to blame . . . for the unhappy relationship which may still exist—between myself and others . . .

Having gone this far in my thinking, my present desire and prayer is to be given the strength of mind and spirit to let go of the past . . .

To let go of any ill feelings toward others . . . which have been injuring me as much if not more than them . . .

And to forgive them as I would be forgiven . . . for what has happened . . .

As I change my attitude and free my mind and heart of these past unhappy experiences . . . I know that my body chemistry is changing for the better . . .

That I am now in better health of mind and body . . .

And that all will be well for me in my future . . .

I therefore thank you, Dear Father, for the Healing Power of FORGIVENESS.

It is FEELING which keeps images alive in Consciousness. If you have reacted positively in favor of the thoughts you just expressed in this meditation, then you have let go of many feelings which could have been disturbing you for some time, perhaps since childhood. When you turn off the feelings for or against any recorded experience, its hold on you is demagnetized and it ceases to exist or have any further effect upon you. In this way, as old images are discarded or outgrown, they die in you and are seldom resurrected.

Actually, countless cells in your body are dying and new cells are being born, just as old ideas in your mind are dying to new thoughts which are replacing them due to your growth in knowledge and experience. A great scientist once said, "The only thing permanent is CHANGE!" You are not exactly the same person you were in body and in mind one second ago!

Now that you have practiced this meditative technique, you can do your own visualizing by picturing whatever you wish to change in your life. Your God-given Creative Power can be given new images to work on.

A fine illustration of the effectiveness of this visualizing method has come to me recently from Ken Garner of Little Rock, Arkansas, who has been following this philosophy since he read my book, *The New TNT-Miraculous Power Within You.* He writes:

Harold, I got the job I was sweating out the last time I talked to you on the phone. I really struggled to keep calm and not get too anxiety-ridden, as you suggested, but it sure was difficult. I wanted this one pretty bad, so I am now the Personnel Administrator for the Arkansas Legislative Counsel (part of the General Assembly) and no longer Personnel Manager for the Department of Finance and Administration. I like the work much more than the previous job and the salary is significantly higher.

I would like you also to know that another of your Mind Control Techniques (picturization) has come to my assistance in a time of need. I read the chapter in *TNT* on excessive appetite control over and over with hope of finding some inspiration and aid in curbing what had become a curse to me—*smoking*. I had attempted so many times to quit and failed as many. I finally realized that if I were ever to quit, I was going to have to look ahead in my mind's eye and picture it already done.

Each evening, I would recount how much and where I had done most of my smoking and struggle to picture it as no longer a part of my life. Slowly but surely the process began to work and I could see myself *not* smoking every time I got on the phone, drank a cup of coffee, ate a meal, etc. These pictured situations began to actualize in my daily life and after approximately five weeks of mental activity, the day arrived when I finished my last pack and never went out for the next one.

I now "see" myself, each day, free from the burdensome tools a smoker is forced to keep around (lighters, ashtrays, cigarettes, etc.) . . . free from the worry of running out, burning your clothes, developing a disease and so on. I am actually enjoying my freedom, too. It has now been six months since I have smoked, and I look forward to a lifetime without them. Your clear and logical assistance in helping me use my own mind properly has been a blessing.

Such testimonies can be repeated many times but this can serve as an example for all to follow who really want to change their life-styles for the better.

We seemingly exist in a boundless sea of thought images, seeking contact with people of similar nature, in accordance with the universal law of mind: like always attracts like. We are alive to whatever we have acquired in consciousness and dead to whatever we have given up. This birth and death process is constantly going on.

You know, of course, that the air around you is saturated with radio and television vibrations—different frequencies of different wavelengths which are converted into sounds and images by the instrumentation of our receiving sets. In much the same manner, myriads of thought waves abound in the "mental ether," emanating from the minds of everyone on this planet—and, quite possibly from the minds of those who have gone on to other dimensions.

As I have previously stated, it is my conviction that your mind is ordinarily protected by what I call a "magnetic insulatory shield" which keeps you from being inundated by energized thought forms which surround you at all times, much as radio and television programs are tuned out and only those received which the operator desires.

This resistance to the possible invasion of external thought forms can be weakened, however, by the use of too much alcohol or drugs, by excessive mental, emotional, and sexual stress, fear, worry, and nervous exhaustion. In such cases, like attracting like, similar imageries from the minds of other humans, known and unknown to you, can attach themselves to your own disturbed imagery and amplify whatever is troubling you at the moment.

It is not too often that people recognize the fusing of their own images with like mental images from other sources. Trained sensitives can be aware of it, and those who have opened their minds unwisely to the reception of impressions received through operation of the Ouija board or through automatic writing. During such practices as these, either uncontrolled functioning of the Subconscious takes over and establishes seeming independent identities, or what would appear to be "earthbound spirit entities" move in to exert "possessive" influences.

Since our minds are actually transmitting and receiving instruments, science has now determined that they can be made susceptible to control, through suggestion or hypnotic forces, either consciously or unconsciously. Diabolical scientists and governments, including our own, have been experimenting—often without the knowledge or consent of selected human subjects—in the development of such control, through use of powerful psychedelic drugs, subliminal imagery, hypnotic and electronic devices, and other persuasive methods. One of the objectives is the creation of subtle means of mesmerizing influential individuals and great masses of people, making them submissive to control and direction.

In this era of pollution of air, land, and water, we now are coming to realize that an even greater danger exists—the possible pollution of our own minds!

Because of their comparative innocence as well as their tendency to imitate and experiment, young children are most apt to be victimized by the suggestive, lurid imagery of pornographic literature and scenes of sex and violence depicted in all media—especially television.

A fifteen-year-old Florida boy entered the house next door, intent on robbery. The home owner, an 82-year-old lady, returned unexpectedly and was shot and killed by him. Charged with murder, the boy's defense attorney attributed the youth's acts to the influence of violent scenes on television. He presented evidence, supported by the family, that the boy spent hours every week, absorbed in the TV shows depicting fiendish acts of violence and murder. He liked to play with guns and to reenact the murderous assaults he had witnessed. His attorney contended that he was rendered temporarily insane, "guilty by reason of TV." Should the judge and jury be convinced that his conduct had been due to the images and urges implanted in his mind by television programs, it can lead to similar defenses in many courts of law.

As I have said, the damage which has been and is being inflicted on the minds of children is astronomical—and it seems that little can be done about it. Public pressure can reduce the number of unsavory, immoral, and savage scenes or series—but enough will remain to continue their harmful influence.

Let me repeat again: Education is the one hope. Young people should be made to see that the shadowy characters committing different violent acts in motion pictures or on TV screens are not real and that they should not try to emulate them by carrying these killing images into real life.

"Something made me do it" is the testimony of many susceptible TV viewers who say that they were impelled to physically reenact a motion picture or TV scene which had been implanted in their minds. They have been made to feel that they are actors playing a part and respond to the urge to duplicate the scene which has been pictorially "scripted" for them. The enactment in real life leaves them with little or no sense of personal responsibility. They feel they really didn't do the deed themselves. Once they have carried out the sexual or violent performance, perpetrated on selected real-life characters, their highly aroused feelings subside and remain quiescent until they build up again when the desire becomes overwhelming to repeat the act. This calls for a new staging of the scene and a new set of characters or victims, conforming as much as possible with a composite of the original TV images.

The most difficult of all images to remove from consciousness are those picturing sexual acts. They are kept alive by the recurring sexual desires of the individual who sees himself, over and over on the motion-picture screen of his mind, performing different sexual acts which are so erotically pleasing that they cause him to seek physical release of these urges at the expense of innocent victims.

This is why a sex criminal remains so dangerous. It is worth repeating what I have had to say in Chapter 5 as a protest against permitting any sex offenders to go free once they have been convicted of crimes against children and older men and women. No matter how long they are incarcerated, much of their time is spent in reliving their sex acts in memory and, once released, these sex images are ready to take over and cause them to seek out new victims, absolutely impervious to any threats of punishment or dire consequences. Outside of hunger, no feeling is stronger than that of sex or more demanding in its imagery.

TO SUMMARIZE:

You are controlled by your FEELINGS which are associated with every IMAGED EXPERIENCE you have had in life.

The strongest feelings always prevail and have the power to attract to you, in time, whatever you image.

When you let go of a feeling for or against something, your image of it loses its power to influence you—and goes back into your memory file, not to be recalled again until this feeling pertaining to it is revived. Your Intellect cannot go against a powerful feeling. Unless you can separate your SENTIMENT from your LOGIC—you will always be persuaded to do things by the dictates of your FEELING rather than your REASON.

The best way to guard against the development and retention of wrong images—either self-created by your reaction to life experiences or implanted in your mind by the projection of destructive images from without—is to take a few minutes' meditative inventory of yourself each night before retirement.

Mentally review the day's happenings and ask yourself if you have formed any images which, if carried in Consciousness can do you harm, in time. Exercise your will to order all feelings of hate and resentment, fear, worry, frustration, repression and the like, and their images, out of your mind.

Appeal to the Higher Power within to guide and protect you. You can learn to be in the world but not of it—and enjoy a comparatively serene, self-confident, healthy, happy day-to-day existence. Start IMAGING it!

CHAPTER 16

How to Image Your Future

For years now, thousands of men and women and young people have written me, testifying to the power of visualization. They have used a simple, basic technique of *imaging* which I have described in one form or another in my different books, the exercise of which has enabled them to magnetically attract to them what they have desired to come to pass.

Before I report some of their experiences and achievements, I would like to present the Meditative Exercise to which they have attributed their successes.

You are to read each statement, individually, and carry out the act or mental attitude indicated, so that you can *feelingly* apply each thought in your Consciousness. Seat yourself in an easy chair. This method for relaxing body and mind can be practiced alone or with members of the family or a study group, repeating and practicing together. It has been performed effectively with an audience of a thousand people, repeating each statement in unison and practicing every step. There is often great power in mass consciousness when everyone is in harmony. But if you feel that some friends or loved ones may not be in sympathy with this method of picturing what you want or need, it is better to conduct your meditative periods alone and in privacy. Don't give anyone the opportunity to distort or change your positive imaging through skepticism or ridicule.

Are you ready? Relax now and repeat to yourself, either aloud or in your mind:

I now relax my body . . .
I make my feet and legs comfortable . . .
I rest my hands and arms in my lap . . .
I let the chair hold my entire weight . . .
I let go of my body with my mind . . .
I leave all fears and worries behind . . .
I feel lighter . . . all physical tension is gone . . .
I close my eyes and shut out the world around me . . .
I turn the attention of my thoughts inward and become unself-conscious of my body . . .
I now feel that I am existing only in my consciousness . . .
A feeling of great inner peace and quiet begins to come over me . . .
In this moment of quiet—of inner stillness—I describe in words and also present in mental picture form . . . what I feelingly desire . . .
If it is better health . . . I picture healing energy permeating every cell and organ of my body . . . renewing and revitalizing it . . .
If I seek new opportunities and achievements . . . whatever they may be . . . I picture myself already having received them . . .
Then, through an exercise of faith . . .
I set up in myself a confident expectation that what I have visualized will come to pass in my outer life . . .
That all the resources and developments I need are on their way to me in time . . .
And that I will be led by my Creative Power and my intuition to be at the right place at the right time . . . protected and guided every day throughout my life.

Practice of this technique of relaxation and visualization can be the key to realization. You do not need to take courses designed to blow you down mentally and emotionally in order to build you up. Some teachings are designed to deflate your ego, to humble you, to knock you out so that you are subservient to the direction of an instructor who plays God in your life. You are reduced to the point of the man in the story who went around hitting himself on the head with a hammer. Asked why he did this, he replied, "Because it feels so good when I stop!"

People do not have to be psychologically punished to remove guilt complexes, frustrations, repressions, and feelings of inferiority, as a means of showing them how to stand up under severe chastisement.

My friend Bob von Gunten of Frederick, Maryland, a psychological counselor, has treated many men and women who have permitted themselves to be browbeaten by often brutal suggestive interrogation, in order to clear up professed wrong mental concepts, and who, once given the all-clear, have found it impossible to come back, and have been shattered by the experience.

"Another thing which disturbs me," states von Gunten, "is the many men and women who end up on my doorstep as the result of so-called psychics, who wrongly have implanted negative thoughts in them, such as 'You will never get married' . . . 'Make out your will right away—your transition is very near.' Statements like these should be criminal offenses. I counsel such men and women to *reject* these kinds of predictions, to depend instead on their own Higher Power within, and send them away with a good dose of *positive thoughts*.

"As for myself, I do not always do as I know I should, but I never quit striving to do better—and I am constantly reminding myself to accept the guidance of my intuition and do as I know I should be doing."

Bob von Gunten knows that it is reasonably easy to maintain the right mental attitude when everything is going right—but the time it really counts is when things have gone wrong and you are able to meet the situation.

Lyn B., of San Jose, California, wrote me a unique

description of how she talked to her Subconscious and told it what she wanted it to do for her. She said she had been interested in ESP since she was about twelve years old but didn't really start to get into it until she was twenty-eight. She had read a number of books and articles on the subject, including some of mine, which she looked upon as interesting phenomena but without substantiation. She continued:

Anyway, I decided around a year ago to stop worrying about my doubts over ESP and accept the fact that it does exist. I reasoned that I would have to have faith in it before it would work for me. Then I laid out an experiment for myself. From now on I would try to use my Subconscious Mind as my "problem solver." I would define the goals to be achieved consciously and pass them on to the Subconscious, often setting a time for when I wanted the answer to "pop up." It was something like a meditation, and I would talk to my Subconscious something like this:

"Now, Subby, I want you to know that I believe in ESP. I want you to start finding all the information and contacts I need to help me solve my problem. I want you to arrange the data and put it in the 'ready file' for me. Since I am employed as a computer systems analyst, I understand how this could be done. I want you to set up a 'buffer region' for incoming messages. I want these messages passed directly to me—in my Conscious Mind —so I can be made aware of them. I also want them 'flagged' as coming from a source that is external to my own mind. I want to be able to observe these messages when they come, and any 'interrupt' of my ordinary thinking will be honored."

I thought this way for about five to ten minutes each evening. On the third day, I started getting messages from the "buffer region." There were a lot of them, most of them too small and of a relatively inconsequential nature. Things like anticipating words, sentences and thoughts in a conversation with friends. But I found that this irritated many people, so I learned to stop *verbalizing*— to keep these impressions to myself—but they still carried the "flag" which I had instructed my Subconscious to tack onto incoming messages.

Well, since then, experiences have continued in a variety of forms. And now I am getting guidance and direction from what I call the "subliminal level" in my everyday life. There is no question but that many of the experiences that are coming to me are outside the bounds of coincidence.

It is almost as though my Subconscious was trying to say to me; "Good grief! I thought you'd never wake up and start using my powers. Now that you have, I'm going to show you some of the range of possibilities."

Some of my friends, noticing a big change in me, are still skeptical. All I say to them is "If you don't believe it, just start trying it. The power is there inside you if you'll learn to tell it what you want it to do for you. Lots of times it will set the stage for you and you will have to act things out, and know how to 'read the script.' There will be other times when you won't get the answers when you think you need them, and you will have to go it alone, doing the best you can, but I have found that things will work out pretty well in due course—better than if I tried to do things all by my conscious self.

This doesn't mean that you won't run into periods of emotional upset and tension. Life seems to be made up of experiences like that. When this happens, it is more difficult to get help from your Subconscious because you don't know just what to ask it to do for you. If you can't direct it properly, it can't do as much for you—it might even attract the wrong things to you. So you've got to make a special effort to keep from being overloaded with fears and worries which start picturing failure and things getting worse instead of better.

My six years' experience, working on computers, taught me a lot about the mind because its operation is somewhat similar. Whatever you feed into it will come out in the same form unless you change the data. I was always highly emotional, and before I could straighten myself out, I went through psychotherapy, which gave me a better understanding of my own mind and how it functions. Developing ESP without benefit of other people's experiences and encouragement is a difficult process. You can easily get off on the wrong track. But when you really learn how to picture what you know is good for you—I have proved that your life has to change for the better.

There is much to be gleaned of value from the experiences Lyn has related and her explanation of the personalized use she has made of her Subconscious Mind. Every individual may have a little different approach. As you have observed, Lyn treated her Subconscious Mind almost as though it was another entity. She addressed it as one would a "faithful servant" and gave it the images of what she wanted, with the confident expectation that the job assigned would be carried out.

Be aware at all times that whatever you are imaging, as you go through life, is being automatically recorded subconsciously and is providing data to be drawn on in some future moment, as needed, to give you answers to oncoming problems and situations.

If you have not done so, resolve to get better acquainted with your Subconscious, to establish personal relations with your Higher Power within—to talk to it in the form of mental pictures—to daydream, if you will, what you would like to do or be or have. See yourself on your "motion-picture screen" as though what you desire has already been accomplished. Have no doubt about it. Know this will all be materialized, produced *for* and *with* you, in *time!*

Age should be no drawback, unless you permit it to be a barrier. So many people, when they have become a little older and have not realized their life ambitions, decide that life has passed them by. Perhaps they cannot do what they once might have done, but other avenues of achievement, of a satisfying nature, can often be open to them, if they will only look for them.

I would like to present now the almost unbelievable account of the achievement of a woman of forty which is illustrative of what can be done by men or women who do not limit themselves by their thinking—who have the courage, faith, and adaptability to enter new fields of endeavor regardless of seeming obstacles and even inexperience. So that you can get the full impact of this life experience, I want you to "hear" the story from Sue Matheis herself, taken from a talk she made. I believe it will carry great inspiration as well as hope for you or anyone who aspires to greater accomplishment in whatever stage of life.

While driving in the car one day, I heard a song on the radio which said in part: "Some men climb a mountain, some men sail the sea. Some men soar into the sky to find what they must be."

Now those words must have been written many years ago, or else they would have added: "Some women soar into the sky to find what they can be." And since this is the Era of the Woman, I'd like to give one woman's experience in finding what she could be . . . but, first, let's take a step back in history.

A little over three score and a dozen years ago, two brothers named Wilbur and Orville had an idea. It was a marvelous idea but when they presented it to their contemporaries, the reaction was "Good idea, Orville . . . but will it get off the ground?"

Until the very recent past, a similar situation existed for women. As we peered through our kitchen curtains at those magnificent men in their flying machines, we too had an idea. But when we mentioned it to the menfolk, they chuckled good-naturedly and gave us fatherly pats on the back—because no one ever thought we'd actually try to fly.

However, they didn't reckon with some of our more courageous and persevering members who took those pats on the back as go-signs and who actually did get off the ground. And now today, women all over the world are taking up airspace. Some men may not be laughing good-naturedly now, but we believe the majority are thrilled that we are sprouting wings.

The skies have literally opened up for women in aviation. It's a fascinating and dynamic world for the young woman who has a lifetime ahead of her. However, there are also those who are already programmed into other endeavors; and even though they agree it would be exciting, they are also mentally sighing; "I'm older, I'm already programmed, the family needs my attention, and Roger would never go for an idea like that."

Well, I was one of those gals. I was older, I had five children, and I was programmed day in day out. Still, I felt that *most* things are possible, that it's *almost* never too late—and yes, that flight as well as life, can begin at *forty*.

Forty seems to be a pretty pivotal age. Researchers tell us that at forty, all women do one of three things: they either gain weight, become alcoholics, or have an affair. What these male researchers neglect to tell us is that we *do* have an alternative. We can get involved in a consuming interest—anything that turns us on—so I thought: Why not try flying?

Flying didn't mean I'd have to give up my kitchen forever—only that I'd add some elastic to my apron strings. Flying didn't mean there would be no more *kaffeeklatsches*—only that I'd meet the girls in a hangar instead of over a kitchen table. And flying didn't mean my family would be advertising for a mother-substitute —only that they'd brag to their friends, "There's no generation gap in our house."

What flying DID do was open up a whole new way of life for me. I found I walked a little faster and I talked a little faster. I not only laughed a lot, but I also cried a lot. But, all told, it was a most positive experience.

To begin with, all you really need is the desire and the opportunity. Oh, a little money wouldn't hurt either, but it's no big deal—as long as you learn the art of extending hamburger over the week so you can afford an afternoon of dual.

I guess I always had the desire to fly but just didn't know it. My opportunity came when my husband signed me up for flying lessons against my will and better judgment. And in just one hour I was completely sky-hooked. It was love at first flight.

Apparently no prior experience or knowledge is necessary to become a pilot because no one could have known less than I about things aeronautical. Planes were completely alien to me, geography had never been one of my favorite subjects, I had no idea there was radio communication between the air and the ground—and the first time I was told to fly a base leg, I didn't know whether to laugh or blush.

But as time flew by, I got my private license, my commercial ticket, and then my instrument rating. My thoughts were constantly focused on flying, and the only reality for me was the flying community. That was where all my kindred spirits were—the freedom lovers, the poets, the adventuresome, the disciplined. Those who got distinct thrills from concentration and perfection.

My husband had created a monster, and he didn't know how to stop her. But he tried! He bought the Riverfront Trolley for me to manage in hopes of getting me back on the programmed track. The Trolley gave happy, narrated tours of the St. Louis riverfront and the immediate downtown area—and I became the "squaw boss" of sometimes as many as eleven men.

Transportation really became a way of life for me. I supervised the Trolley six days a week, ferried planes on the seventh and sandwiched car pools in between. Sort of a modern version of Woman and Her Spinning Wheels.

Life was certainly full at this point but, like flying, it had its ups and downs. Learning to study again was quite an ordeal, especially when it had to be sandwiched in among so many other obligations. And sometimes the kids had picklepusses when the services to which they had become accustomed were no longer forthcoming.

But those lows were balanced against the highs. Like the very glorious moment when you solo for the first time—when you're scared to death and yet thrilled to death. Or coming out the winner from a forced landing. If I needed excitement, I got it from ferrying planes across unfamiliar territory, without radios and almost always in marginal weather. That's when I not only laughed a lot and cried a lot, but also prayed a lot.

I'm reminded of one Sunday morning when I was hugging the countryside, slithering between menacing black storms, raindrops falling on my head—and I thought: How ridiculous! Why am I battling all this when I could be safely asleep in a church pew or basting a Sunday chicken? But of course I knew the answer at the end of the flight when I conquered a fear, met a challenge, and came out unscathed to boot.

Well, every activity has to lead someplace, and I started flying announcers for the KMOX Radio Traffic Watch.

After about six months, opportunity knocked again and I was asked to assist Officer Don Miller in reporting traffic on Friday afternoons. I would be known as "Sue in 'Copter Two."

That first traffic watch was quite a story, and it would take a long time to make it short. But I was catapulted into the job with only five minutes' notice and absolutely no training in the field of communications. It was quite a surprise, and you would have laughed had you seen the struggle that ensued in the cockpit as the headset was placed on me, and I took it off, and it went on again.

Thank goodness pilot-training, and wife-training and mother-training make one flexible. And so I flexed. And it was really neat because directing traffic is, after all, a natural for women. Haven't we been accused of "backseat driving" all through the ages?

But the really spiffy part is, not only do I get a chance to tell the men where to go, but they listen—and I get paid for it!

As for no previous training in the field of communications? Well, that was really no problem either. We women were communicating our thoughts long before the telephone and telegraph. And, as Officer Don Miller likes to remind me: When God plucked a rib from Adam, he made the first loudspeaker.

For those who may insist that flying will get you nowhere, I'd like to say that with a little bit of luck, and some help from your friends, it will not only take you from Point A to Point B—but beyond.

For instance, because of flying, I was fortunate enough to win a thousand-dollar scholarship for the Whirly Girls (an international organization of licensed women helicopter pilots)—and with that help I earned my commercial helicopter rating—the first to be issued to a woman by the State of Missouri. And that's not all.

Because of flying, KMOX Radio, St. Louis, opened the door to the world of radio to me. Not only do I do traffic and news reporting, but I also prepare and air features of my own choosing.

But the most important thing flying has done is—it makes me look forward to each new day. It has shown me that ANYTHING is possible, it's NEVER too late and that flight—as well as life—can begin at *forty!*

What a great human experience—and what a glorious testimony to the power of thought—of IMAGING what you want to do—of persevering with courage, with faith and application—and the GOOD THINGS which keep on happening as you keep your mind on TARGET!

CHAPTER 17

How to Create a Better Self-Image

Image building and image changing seem to be the popular order of the day.

Manufacturers are constantly striving to improve the image of their products so that they can be made more attractive and appealing to customers. The center of the image-making industry is the Madison Avenue advertising community. Millions of dollars are being spent each year in new selling slogans, new designs of merchandise, new color combinations, new packaging, new smells, new tastes, new sounds, new eye-catching devices, new feeling sensations, new features in every commodity or serviceable line, all for the purpose of implanting more luring buying images in people's minds.

Merchandisers know the suggestibility as well as the gullibility of human nature. They are quick to take advantage of it when an Elvis Presley or an Evil Knievel or a Kojak or a Joe Namath or a *Star Wars* movie appears on the scene by creating and launching a line of shirts, pants, boots, football helmets, outer-space suits, records, guns, toys, and what not, associated with colorful personalities and events that have captured public fancy at the moment.

Image creators in the advertising fraternity take great care to picture only that which has the right appeal or makes the right impression. Their main aim is to instill images in your mind which will give you a compelling urge to buy. The handling of a presidential campaign is a case in point. Every factor concerning the appearance of a candidate is analyzed. Is he wearing the right kind and color of suits and ties? Are his hairdos and makeup complimentary? How about his posture and his facial expressions, his manner of speaking, his ability to communicate the proper warmth as well as his apparent sincerity and authority?

If the candidate is not naturally endowed with certain desirable qualities, they must be simulated. The public must be given the image that he is all things to all people of all ages: a man of the people. Speechwriters must give him the right things to say, create headline-catching comments. Insofar as is possible, he must never be caught off guard on unscheduled interviews or contacts with the voters without having a calculated response. He can easily change a public image of himself as Wendell Willkie once did when he laughed off a statement he had made as "just so much campaign oratory."

How deeply you feel for or against an image of a person, an advertised product, or an idea determines the degree of its influence upon you at any given time. All images in your mind are ready to respond on an instant's notice, magnetized into action as your attention is attracted or directed to them.

Whatever you give reality to in your mind, whether it is imagined or an actual experience, becomes an indistinguishable part of you. If the images are of a disturbed and distorted nature, they cannot change as long as you continue to harbor them with similar thoughts and feelings. This fact must be impressed upon you time and again.

Fred M. Banks is president of The Oneness Foundation, P.O. Box 677, Spring, Texas, an organization dedicated to the development of Total Self-Sufficiency. He has given me permission to quote his thoughts on the acquirement of a "Powerful Positive Self-Image" from the foundation's bulletin:

Have you often wondered how some people practically always obtain and realize their highest dreams and goals without really trying? Some people just naturally have that certain something that it takes to be successful, while others can spend a lifetime chasing endless rainbows, never finding success and contentment.

Why are there such differences in people? Why are some successful and some not? Why do some people set goals, and some, unfortunately, do not? Why? Why? WHY? The never-ending list of whys . . .

It is my belief that to be successful or really happy and completely satisfied with the mainstream of life, a *positive self-image* must be achieved before anything else.

How is this done?

How can we develop a positive self-image?

The best way is to begin to seek and to recognize the positive aspects of life.

Is life itself positive? Do you get a positive feeling living in this country? Is it positive to wake up each morning and greet the sunrise?

If you will check the list of positives, you will find that they far outweigh the negatives. Have you thanked God for life? You are one of His good creations. Do you appreciate this fact?

Having realized the positive aspects of life, you should then give thought to your own personal positive aspects.

You must know and believe that you are positive and can do positive things. That so long as you can maintain a positive mental image, you can overcome all of life's obstacles. Not one-half of them, not most of them, but ALL of them.

You are depressed because you expect to be depressed; you are sick because you expect to be sick; you are negative because you have permitted yourself to be influenced by negative things surrounding you. You criticize because others do it, although most of the time you may not be sure of what you are criticizing.

You can escape from all of these negative conditions by looking for the positive aspects in all people, places and things, as well as in yourself. Do this and life will suddenly hold great rewards for you. Think about all the real treasures that can and do exist for you. They are not in the form of silver and gold or material things—but things that cannot be bought at any price such as health, sunshine, happiness, love, friends—all God-given, if you will only reach out and accept them.

This is what a positive self-image can do for you.

By now you should be fairly well convinced of the influence that all images of your reaction to past experiences are continuing to live on in the attitudes you have toward present and future happenings.

The image of yourself which you present to the world, to those who know you, and to yourself, is the result of your past thoughts and feelings toward any subject that may be brought up or any situation you may face. You may try to conceal or repress how you really feel about some things in your life—but what you *do* reveal or *do not* restrain is what you are, at the moment, in the estimation of others.

Your wife or husband or friend may say to you, on occasion: "You don't seem to be yourself today," and this may be true, if you have varied from an ordinarily established "norm" as to personality expression. We are all creatures of moods and feel better or worse, physically and mentally and emotionally at different times, dependent on our reaction to whatever is happening to us.

Study yourself in the mirror. What is the physical image that you see? Has Nature endowed you with pleasing features? Trying to see yourself as others see you, do you feel you can do something to improve your appearance? If you do, get busy doing it! Your eyes can be the most expressive. Are they warm and kindly and direct, as you look into them? Do you think you would like a person like yourself? Do you get a friendly feeling from this image of yourself? Are you always pretty much like this—or is your face often contorted by disturbed, unhappy expressions? Do you smile naturally, or do you find that smiles do not come easily? Do you greet everyone the same way—or do you reserve special greetings for special people, and "give out" only when you feel like it? Or when you are meeting someone on whom you wish to make a definite impression?

These are all telltale evidences of what you really are—the true image of your outer expression. You may not have thought it too important, but you are projecting your image to everyone with whom you come in contact, in a close or passing way, and they carry this image of you with them in their minds.

In that great song, "Some Enchanted Evening," composed by Rodgers and Hammerstein, the impact of an attractive image is poignantly dramatized in these lines:

"Some enchanted evening . . . you may see a stranger . . .
Across a crowded room . . .
And somehow you know even then . . .
That somehow you'll see her again and again . . .
Some enchanted evening . . . someone may be laughing . . .
You may hear her laughing . . .
Across a crowded room . . ."

And the song goes on to say,
"The sounds of her laughter will sing in your dreams!"

In our post office, in the little town of Mountain View, Arkansas, there is an enchanting young lady who is the inspiring embodiment of the woman in this song. As neighbors and strangers enter, the whole post office lights up as Nancy greets each one with a cheery "Hi! How are you? Everything all right?" There is nothing put on—it is a natural personality expression. There is a radiance in her eyes—she is just so glad to see everyone. She makes no distinction, young or old. All receive the same warmth, the same personal attention. She knows almost everyone in the county and everyone knows her, and loves her. Some people say, "Thanks, Nancy—just seeing you has made my day!" When they leave, Nancy's smile and her voice follows them with "Have a good day!" Never have we seen a person quite like her, and how we wish that everyone could project such a spirit of good feeling at all times. What a wonderful world this would be!

Yes, the way you project your self-image counts! Could your very presence attract attention "across a crowded room" or of anyone in any place? Could the sound of your laughter lighten someone else's day? It costs so little to show an interest in another person, friend or stranger. It all depends upon the kind of image you are naturally transmitting.

Some years ago, when I realized the value of creating the right image, and the fact that thoughts could be transmitted and received, I formed the practice of visualizing in advance what I would do and say at a forthcoming interview with an important person. If it was an appointment with an individual I had never met, and I had a proposal to make to him or her, I pictured the meeting and suggested to myself that I would be inspired to make the right get-acquainted approach and that I would present my thoughts in a manner which would be acceptable. When I had done this, I would make my mind receptive while I let myself "listen" to any possible resistance. If I sensed opposition to my proposal, I would try to determine its nature and then call forth a satisfying answer which I felt would close the interview in my favor. Once this was accomplished, I cut short the meditation, with the inner confidence that when the time came for the actual appointment, everything would turn out as visualized. Invariably, I would find myself saying the right things at the right time and the conference would be concluded successfully. This was largely due, I believe, to my having conducted this interview mentally beforehand, on subconscious levels, with the mind or minds of the individuals concerned. In any event, you will find that it will help immensely for you to adopt this visualizing means of preparing to meet and deal with people.

When two people share the same experiences, the images of these experiences blend and they become one in spirit. If any disturbances or misunderstandings occur, these images of a harmonious relationship become distorted, often leading to physical, mental, and emotional upsets. As long as one person or the other holds a resentful image in mind, toward his or her mate, their former harmonious relationship cannot be restored.

Married couples should never go to bed with a hateful image of the other in mind. If they do, their Subconscious Minds will work on it during the night and they will usually awaken feeling more irritable and antagonistic than before. Occasionally they will live, unspeaking, under the same roof for days or weeks, each resolved not to be the first to apologize, ask forgiveness, or offering to make amends. People who are plagued by an uncontrollable temper—and there are many—can destroy all images of love and respect in time.

"I don't know what gets into me," a highly refined and intelligent woman said to me, "but care of the children becomes so burdensome, at times, that I have lost my temper and not only punished them too severely, but have taken my feelings out on my husband when he has come home. I have even found myself regretting that I had ever married, and wondering if I had really loved John. What in the world is happening to me? I'm afraid, if this keeps on, it is going to develop such hostility between us that it will lead to a breakup. John's feelings are also on edge. Little things he says and does irritate me, and I find myself suspicious of his motives. For example, he remarked recently that it was a nice day, and I thought that was his way of trying to run my life by suggesting that I should do the washing—when it wasn't in his mind at all. So you can see how we are getting on each other's nerves—and our images of each other are changing. We do not feel the same toward each other as we once did."

This is a simple example of the manner in which the "love image" can turn about and become a "hate image" —and all the remembered faults of a husband and wife, once forgiven, forgotten, overlooked or adjusted to, can be so magnified that they are no longer bearable.

To create and preserve the best possible image of oneself, I have practiced a meditation period each night before retiring which has been helpful to me and should be equally helpful to you. I take a few minutes to review the outstanding happenings of the day while trying to see myself as others may have seen me. This sort of objectivity enables me to evaluate whether or not I have given as good an account of myself as I might in my association with others.

It is so easy to become self-centered, to overlook opportunities to be more thoughtful and considerate, to be mindful of the needs and interests of friends and loved ones. Of course, no life can be lived without mistakes in judgment, without occasional arguments and disagreements, without some painful experiences—but I have found that I must take a few moments each day to reflect upon these happenings and make a corrective adjustment to them; if not these images will tend to attract more of the same kinds of attitudes and experiences to me in my future.

I have come to look forward to these nightly inventories as the time to get right with myself, to clear the deck, so to speak, of the "mental garbage" I may have picked up in the course of events, and to dump it out of my Consciousness by facing up to what I now recognize as useless and even harmful thoughts and feelings.

Sometimes I find the process painful as I think back over unhappy incidents with others in which I have reacted wrongly, as I now realize, and am still holding resentful or disturbed thoughts about them. I well know, from past experience, that unless I cleanse my mind of these memories, unless I forgive others and myself for what has happened, no matter who has been more at fault, that these mental images will upset my body chemistry in time and contribute to the development of possible physical illnesses.

Then, when I have mentally surveyed these past thoughts and acts, I take a few minutes to place new images in my mind of what I now know I should have said and done. I then resolve that the next time I may face a similar situation or experience, I will meet it in a more constructive way so that I will have nothing to correct or adjust or regret in any future dealings with others.

The time has now come for me to focus my attention

on the things I have planned for the next day and the days following. Whatever I am working on or dreaming of, I see myself, in my mind's eye, attracting to me the right conditions, circumstances, resources, opportunities, experiences, and people to help bring what I am visualizing to pass. What I am really doing is projecting the image of myself into the future and picturing myself achieving success in my personal and business life.

This meditation may take fifteen minutes each night or whatever time is required. I drop off to sleep with a feeling of mental and physical relief, free of tensions. My Consciousness is cleared of all disturbing or conflicting thoughts and the creative power of mind has been given blueprints, in picture form, to help reproduce these images in my Outer World.

What you visualize in your meditations does not always begin to manifest as soon as you might expect or desire. You might be disposed to lose interest or faith. I have had people write me and say that they have been picturing things they wanted for some weeks and nothing has happened. It's increasingly difficult to believe in something which is showing no evidence of starting to happen. Are they doing something wrong? Some of them report that they are having a hard time "seeing" themselves in their mind's eye. How clearly should they see it—and if they can't see it, will it do any good to keep on meditating?

Good questions! I repeat again: some people are natural visualizers—it is easy for them to image what they want. Others are what I call the "feeling type." They can feel what they desire very strongly, even though they find it difficult to create images. The results will be the same because the Creative Power will take what they see or feel—or both—and go to work on it. I tell some people that they are trying too hard—trying to force things to happen—and when they are doing this, it means that they are afraid what they are picturing won't happen and they have to help it along by giving it a mental push. Actually, however, they are placing a picture of doubt in their minds, and this will produce just the opposite effect desired. Just imagine what would happen if you took a picture with a camera and opened the camera to see if it was developing! Once you have impressed the image of what you want on the *film* of your mind, wait patiently and with confidence to let it be developed in due course of time. You can repeat your picturing each day or night to more deeply impress it on your Subconscious, but don't force it—just see and know that you are going to be given the right guidance to take the right steps and do the right things to help materialize your image or images into real-life experiences and achievements.

Here now are some powerful Positive Affirmations which if repeated each night before retiring, along with such other meditations as you feel the need, will help create as perfect a SELF-IMAGE as you can hope to develop. Listen to your own voice in the privacy of your own home or inner office or wherever you choose to meditate, as you hear yourself say, with resolute feeling:

I will never compare myself unfavorably with another human being . . .

I know now that I possess within myself . . . the power to become a more interesting, appealing personality . . .

In my own right . . . I know, too, that no individual . . . whatever he may think of me or do to me . . . has the power to hurt me—unless I let him hurt me . . .

Knowing this, difficult as it may sometimes be . . . I will return kindness for any word or act . . .

Which might previously have aroused hatred or resentment within me . . .

I refuse to permit myself to get upset emotionally when things go wrong . . .

Or to imagine that I do not possess the ability in myself . . . with God's help . . . to meet whatever happens . . .

Realizing that the best way I can serve myself is to serve others . . .

I will look each day for opportunities to help my friends and loved ones . . .

I will never more lose faith in God or myself

Because I know that this faith . . .

Is my ever-present protection . . .

Guide and strength . . .

In every moment of need . . .
This is my resolution and my prayer . . . Amen.

Always remember, your most priceless possession is the nature and character of your SELF-IMAGE! It always reflects what you really are and to a great degree determines your success in life—the appeal and influence you have upon all friends and loved ones and acquaintances—and how they feel toward you.

You are projecting this IMAGE of yourself at all times—and, as it changes, due to any change in your mental and emotional attitudes, so do conditions change around you.

Your PERSONALITY is a vital part of your SELF-IMAGE, as is your PHYSICAL APPEARANCE. How you walk, how you talk, how you act under different situations and associations, every movement of your body, every facial expression—they are all communicating—leaving a visual, auditory, and feeling impression on others—forming IMAGES of you in their minds.

You don't need to be self-conscious about it—just realize that you have the power, at all times, through the simple, natural process of being YOURSELF—to reach and favorably influence everyone!

CHAPTER 18

The Images of an Afterlife

What is your image of Death?

Do you see Death as an "end-all" existence when you will never again be conscious of Self, when the identity that gives you an "I am I" awareness ceases at the moment your physical body is no more?

If this is your vision or feeling, then it is having an effect upon your attitude toward life, and even upon your body chemistry. You cannot be looking toward the future with basic assurance and expectation. To be constantly visualizing everything you have achieved and experienced and loved as reduced to little or nothing when your time comes to die is a devitalizing thought picture—and your Creative Power within, in obedience to this limiting blueprint, tends to produce for you what you are picturing—a seeming *oblivion*.

Today, however, it is my conviction based on years of research and experimentation, as well as the testimony of many men and women who have had what they believe to have been "afterlife" experiences, that there is human survival after Death. If this is true, then it should be obvious that a "death ends all" attitude can be severely handicapping to such a person when he arrives on the Other Side. We know, beyond a doubt, that our images of Self pretty much dictate what we are in this life, and we can expect them to determine the nature of our consciousness and our existence in what we call the Next Dimension.

Two medical doctors, Elisabeth Kubler-Ross and Raymond Moody, Jr. in their books, *On Death and Dying* and *Life After Life* have presented provocative and convincing evidence that men and women, pronounced clinically dead, on recovering consciousness, have told of adventures in an "Afterlife" in which they found themselves in places of beauty and activity and where they were greeted by loving friends and relatives—experiences so real and inviting that they had been reluctant to return to earth.

If you can find it possible to accept their testimony, or if you have had your faith in an Afterlife cemented by experiences of your own, then you will have been given sufficient conviction to bridge the "image gap" between this life and the next, so that you can begin to look forward to the existence beyond with fearless anticipation. No mental attitude that you can ever acquire can mean so much to you and your future, when you will one day face a transition from your residence in this body form to another state of being, which will seem just as real to you there as this existence has been to you here.

As you can see, imagery evidently plays a vital part at the moment of transition. Many people describe the sensation of passing through a dark, tunnellike area and seeing an inviting bright light at the end of this tunnel, to which they are irresistibly drawn. It would seem that birth into a next existence must follow the pattern of transiting through a type of vaginal canal. Such experiences do not happen to everyone, of course, and this is one of the mysteries. Why should some people at the apparent moment of death be favored with such transcendent and spiritually rewarding and reassuring experiences, and not others?

It is possible, though this does not always apply, that the conscious or unconscious attitude of the individual toward Death has a bearing on the reaction he or she will have toward leaving this life.

My grandmother, Mary Morrow, aged eighty-two, on the verge of death, was brought out of a coma by the emotionalized entreaties of her grown daughter, Flora, who cried, "Mother, you mustn't leave me. I can't do without you!"

When grandmother became conscious, she reproved Flora by saying, "Why did you call me back? It was my time to go—it was so peaceful and wonderful there." She lived a year longer, and when a now-fatal illness came upon her, she called Flora to her bedside and said, "Flora, you must free my spirit—let me go this time."

"All right, mother," said Flora, "if it is your wish."

Grandmother smiled, patted her hand with a quiet "thank you," and as she closed her eyes for the last time on earth, was heard to say, "I see them—the dear ones are waiting for me."

Were these merely images or were they actual views of the Next Life? And is this Next Existence just beyond our five physical senses, nearer to us than we are ordinarily aware?

A. J. Loriaux, a friend of mine who lost his beloved wife Wilma three years ago—and had been tempted to join her by suicide—after some months of experimentation, finally felt that he was receiving tape-recorded messages through her spirit voice. This method of communication was not too satisfactory, but his great desire to get through to her eventually activated a psychic sense which enabled him to establish a two-way telepathic contact, in which he heard her voice above his left ear and developed the ability to carry on a conversation with her as though by telephone.

I have carefully investigated this phenomenon and am convinced it is genuine—that somehow A. J. has developed an amazing psychic faculty. I have sat beside him as he converses with his wife Wilma—whose voice I do not hear—but whose answers to questions by A. J. or me are instant, direct, and believable.

A. J. had been an accomplished organist but had lost his interest in the instrument with Wilma's death—and had sold it. She reproved him for having done this, telling him she had provided him with a duplicate of his organ in the home she had prepared for him, which he would enjoy when his time came to join her. She explained that they could create whatever they desired where she was—that they were living in a "thought world."

Reality or imagery or wishful thinking? So much we do not know. Do we take images of what we would like to have achieved on earth and find we possess a creative power which can make these images take form in what we call the Next Dimension? Both the good and the bad?

Juan Garcia Paniagua, a pilot in the Mexican Air Force during the Second World War, told me of an experience he had when his plane was falling out of control and he was facing what he felt to be imminent death. There suddenly flashed before his Consciousness, as though he was viewing life-sized scenes from a motion picture, different experiences of his past life. As nearly as he could recall, there were about twenty of these highly vivid and emotional images. He could see and feel himself reliving these experiences, all of which took place within a few seconds but seemed to have lasted longer in another time dimension. At the last minute, as though by a miracle, the plane leveled off as it was about to crash, and he managed to land it on the edge of an airstrip, unharmed.

Giving thanks to his merciful deliverance by some Higher Power, almost as though God had extended a protective hand, Juan said he had ever since believed in Divine guidance. There are countless accounts like this from men and women, who, almost at the moment of death, have relived their lives.

This indicates that everyone possesses what might be termed a "videotape recording" of all past images, which can be triggered or played back, either in sequence or spasmodically by some new experience in which the existence of the entity itself is threatened. Something starts the reel of the mind to spinning—and the past life events seem to be assembling for some future use by the entity in whatever state it might find itself to be.

In our psychic probes of Jupiter, Mercury, and Mars, Ingo Swann and I received "feedback images" of conditions which we felt existed on these planets. Can we glimpse conditions even more readily when we arrive in the "heaven worlds," as well as create what we want to see and experience?

An army officer was being invalided home with his wife by plane from Japan. He died before the plane landed in the States. His wife was pregnant at the time, and the baby was born seven months later. One night, as she was sitting near the baby's bed, she told the baby how much she wished his father could have seen him. She was startled by a voice beside her which said, "I *am* seeing him, Gloria!" Looking around, she saw the figure of her husband, attired in his army uniform sitting on the bed next to her. It seemed so natural that she accepted his image as though he was still alive. They had a little visit, when he said he was sorry, he couldn't stay longer—but he would always be with her. And with that, he was gone. Then the wife, suddenly realizing what had happened, went screaming downstairs to tell a woman roomer and, as she later reported, "scared the living daylights out of her."

Image or actual spirit presence? Had the wife slipped into the Next Dimension, or what is called the Astral World? Did she exist on the "same wavelength" with her loved one for a time? Perhaps there is no adequate explanation—except to testify that these things actually occur.

It is the unexpected, unsought times when apparitions appear, that offer the greatest opportunity for speculative evaluation. I have had flashes of feeling, on occasion, when I have felt the presence of a friend or loved one who is no longer on earth. Whenever this happens, which is seldom, I always make my mind receptive and try to receive whatever messages the presence might be seeking to impart.

Impressions usually come to me in the form of images or mental pictures which I must interpret in my own words. Sometimes, in the absence of images, I receive strong feelings which soon lead to visual sensations. Basic communication appears to be dependent upon the mind's ability to "see" in order to understand.

I have often been asked if due to my sensitivity, I have made an organized effort to contact the minds of those who have passed on. It has long been my conviction that those in the Next Dimension are as busily occupied in the life there as though they had taken up residence in some other part of this earth, from whence they could not return, and we would not ordinarily make contact—until we might be able to make the journey to them.

Recently, however, it appears that organized efforts are being made by those on the Other Side, to help us develop ways and means for establishing scientifically recognized instruments of communication. Our ESP Research Associates Foundation in Little Rock, Arkansas, is planning to set up an extensive Survival After Death research program and to invite the assistance of genuine psychics and spirit mediums, from around the world, in experiments, together with a greater scientific study of the tape recording of so-called spirit voices, and the photographing of seeming spirit forms or projected mental images.

If absolute evidence could be secured that we survive death, and will find ourselves in a world at least as real as this world (if not of a higher order), I personally feel that it would dramatically change the attitude of all mortals toward others and themselves. If we could know for a certainty that life is not cheap and expendable, that it possesses a value beyond this short existence, that we are being prepared by our experiences on this planet for an existence beyond this—it should cause us to pay more attention to our behavior here—especially if HOW we think and feel should be discovered to be developing what I call our "spirit gravity"—and which will determine the level of existence to which our gravitation may lead us.

It has been pretty well established that like always attracts like in the realm of mind, which could explain, if there should be so-called "earthbound areas" in the Next Dimension, why many undeveloped persons in this life will find themselves confined in temporary residence, until they are able to be helped, informed, and thus equipped to "raise their vibrations" by seeking and acquiring spiritual development.

In this life we observe that our degree of intelligence and refinement pretty well dictates our position in Society, and we tend to gravitate to people and environments which relate to others in the same state of development or undevelopment. It would seem that the same laws of evolution would prevail wherever we might find ourselves to exist. This could be called The Law of Compensation, which has long been regarded as a control factor in human life.

The image of ourselves is actually of utmost importance—and we cannot rise above the level of whatever concept we have of ourselves until we have been able to change the image.

The religionists would say that the only way we can "save our souls" is to develop a "spiritual awareness." But it has become more and more apparent that no one can do this for us. We are crucifying ourselves by our own wrong thinking and wrong actions—and their effects cannot be removed by any force outside ourselves, however much we might desire an "easy way out."

There is a Higher Power within us, but it does not compel us to think right. It simply responds to whatever we picture for it. It is constantly reproducing or attempting to reproduce the IMAGE we hold, at the moment, of what we wish to do or be or have—and letting us grow through experience. In so doing, we are developing our "spirit gravity" and attracting better and better things to us as we raise the level of our thinking. In this way, we are preparing for our future, not only in this life but the life to come.

In any event, these are my thoughts and concepts—which you must test and prove for yourself, through the experiences you are having.

Assuming there is an Afterlife, what, then, can you be expected to take with you when death occurs? Taking for granted that your Unknown Creator has provided you with a higher vibrating body form for your existence in the Next Dimension, it is apparent that you survive with only your conscious awareness of your Identity. If your identity —the "I am I" of you continues to exist—it must have been accompanied by your Memory—because without Memory, your awareness of a past life on earth is obliterated and you would be, to all intents and purposes, in a state of oblivion. A preservation of the IMAGE of who you are is essential to Self-Conscious survival.

There is increasing evidence, however, that Memory and Identity *do* survive—and that those who have made the transition *do* retain a feeling for friends and loved ones who are left temporarily on earth. In the times when they have tried, or been able to manifest their continued existence and interest, they indicate that they have a way of knowing what those on earth are experiencing and, as proof of their identity, can also recall incidents which have happened when they were still residents on this planet.

What we do not know for a fact, we can only conjecture. We do know, however, that as the Bible has stated, "We are fearfully and wonderfully made," that the body is a remarkably sensitized instrument, that the Intelligence in us which operates the body possesses depth and capacities that we haven't begun to develop and express as yet, and that we apparently have been programmed by our unthinkably great Creator for a destiny which is beyond our life on this planet, in higher vibrating realms which we can only faintly image in the timeless time yet to come—as we hopefully view what seems to be an endless evolution ahead of us.

Perhaps this is all inevitably leading toward the Ultimate Reality and when we arrive there in some far-distant time—who knows—we may find ourselves launched upon a Spiritual Journey to a new and even greater Reality.

Let's IMAGE that, at any rate, we carry with us the daily awareness that we are living in ETERNITY now!

Epilogue

For years, at different times when I have sought answers to profound questions of a mental and spiritual nature that have not been forthcoming through ordinary thought processes, the answers have occasionally come out of a sleep state, requiring that I get up immediately and write them down, or call upon Martha to record them for me as I have dictated at high speed so that these onrushing thoughts would not escape me.

This is what happened on completion of this book, *Picture What You Want*. I had laid the manuscript aside as a finished work when this Inner Experience came to me—and with it the feeling that it had been designed as a Final Summation.

I believe you will find it provocative, as I have, and that it somehow belongs in the realm of your thinking, as you continue your search for greater knowledge of Self.

The Universe is an immense Image of the God Mind, and we are an infinitesimal, but still significant and evolving part of this God Image.

As God evolves with man, the image changes—and this change is, and has been, never-ending. Everything appears to be progressing from the inexpressibly lower

217

to the inconceivably higher, and we seem to exist in a sea of Consciousness with countless levels.

Where thoughts come from, what thoughts are, and where thoughts go is a mystery. They are particles of spinning energy, given shape and direction by the "I am I" in us as they seek union with other thought forms vibrating on the same wavelength. Like is forever attracting like in the restless realm of mind.

Each thought has a life and identity of its own. When new associations or experiences reveal a thought form to be false or no longer usable by the entity, it is discarded or changed and loses its identity. Soul is the "I am I" identity, and Spirit is the gift of Life which sustains it. Soul and Spirit are therefore synonymous and inseparable.

A constantly accumulating aggregation of magnetically charged thought forms are revolving about the ego or identity or "I am I" presence. It has access to any one or more of them as needed, and the identity's awareness continually shifts from concentration upon one thought form or another. These thought forms take possession of Consciousness momentarily and contribute the intelligence or concept contained in them to the ego as needed.

Science describes this functioning as related to the several billions of brain cells which are acting as miniature files for containment of these myriads of thought forms. Almost computerlike, they leave their cellular pigeon-holes—glow in consciousness for the time they are needed to serve the entity—and then return to their residence in the intricate, cellular network system, awaiting another call for use by the entity. There is a duplicate recording in the astral or spirit body as well as the physical memory system.

When nervous breakdowns occur, thought forms are out of order. The images distort, superimpose, run riot. The ego loses control. Thought forms of invading discarnate entities merge with the thought forms of the living mortal, serve to amplify them and give urges to the ego— which is often unable to resist or control them.

The invading entity thereupon participates vicariously with the living mortal in sex acts or other activities. This attachment is often maintained—its influence coming and going—so that the living entity may lose his identity and exist in a confused state. He seems to remember past lives which belong instead to the invading discarnate.

Once given birth and projected from mind, thought forms are kept alive in the magnetic field and are spinning about in the mental ether seeking new opportunities for identification with other minds. A scientist, seeking new invention ideas, may draw into the orbit of his mind a thought form which has originated from other minds—living or dead—which can solve his problem. Conversely, an individual whose mind is beset with strong sexual urges, can magnetically attract similar thought forms which become attached and are given new life by the living mortal.

This is a thought-form universe. A thought—as nearly as can be described—is a globular, encapsulated, magnetized image of anything that can be conceived by mind. It can exist by itself or be related to clusters of thought forms—each contributing their bit to any whole idea or feeling. Without thought forms or mental images, there can be no awareness of being. In the absence of thought forms, there would be no consciousness.

A shock treatment is designed to break up a fixation on one thought or feeling. This shatters the mental block for the time being until the thought forms reassemble in an orderly manner and a person's so-called entity is restored.

Mind must always have a target to focus upon. It can be a series of incidental interests or some major concerns— but an individual's every waking moment has to be centered upon something. If a person is deprived of outside interests, his mind's attention turns back upon itself and, unless relieved, can bring about mental and emotional disorders. Few people can long stand a focusing on Self.

The Self is not comfortable unless it is focused on something outside of Self. That is why adepts—people who have acquired high spiritual development—stress the virtue and importance of the Selfless Life.

We were apparently created to be of service to others and, in so doing, to lead a Selfless Life and find the Real Self.

Man's basic fear is that of Self. He loses this fear to the degree that he can lose himself in the service of others.

ESP RESEARCH ASSOCIATES FOUNDATION,

For exploration of the origin and nature of man's sixth sense

SUITE 1630, UNION NATIONAL PLAZA
LITTLE ROCK, ARKANSAS 72201

HAROLD SHERMAN
Founder and Board Chairman

To You Who Have Read This Book

It would be helpful to the research work our Foundation is doing if you would report to us some of the unusual experiences you have had through exercising the power of Visualization—picturing what you have wanted to do or be or have in life.

It would also be of inspiration to others to have the assurance, as a result of your experiences, that these higher powers of mind, rightly used, do work.

My thanks in advance for your cooperation. If you would like a reply, please enclose return postage.

My BEST always.

Harold Sherman

NON-FICTION

☐	BED/TIME/STORY—Robinson	X2540	1.75
☐	EIGHT IS ENOUGH—Braden	23002-3	1.75
☐	FELTON & FOWLER'S BEST, WORST & MOST UNUSUAL—Felton & Fowler	23020-1	1.95
☐	HOLLYWOOD TRAGEDY—Carr	22889-4	1.95
☐	THE INTRUDERS—Montandon	22963-7	1.95
☐	THE WOMAN SAID YES—West	23128-3	1.95
☐	ANN LANDERS SPEAKS OUT	13946-8	1.75
☐	IT'S ALL IN THE STARS—Zolar	13566-7	1.75
☐	MOON MADNESS—Abel	13697-3	1.75
☐	THE PSYCHIC POWER OF ANIMALS—Schul	13724-4	1.75
☐	THE SECRET POWER OF PYRAMIDS—Schul & Pettit	X3273	1.75
☐	FROM PLATO TO NIETZCHE—Allen *(Former title Guide Book to Western Thought)	Q768	1.50
☐	THE PSYCHIC POWER OF PYRAMIDS—Schul & Pettit	90001-0	3.95

Buy them at your local bookstores or use this handy coupon for ordering:

Please allow 4 to 5 weeks for delivery. This offer expires 1/79.

BESTSELLERS

MODERN CLASSICS

☐	THE ASSASSINS—Oates	23000-7	2.25
☐	WONDERLAND—Oates	22951-3	1.95
☐	MARRY ME—Updike	23369-3	1.95
☐	A MONTH OF SUNDAYS—Updike	C2701	1.95
☐	THE CHOSEN—Potok	23495-9	1.95
☐	IN THE BEGINNING—Potok	22980-7	1.95
☐	WOMAN ON THE EDGE OF TIME —Piercy	23208-5	2.25
☐	GILES GOAT BOY—Barth	23524-6	2.50
☐	CHIMERA—Barth	23152-6	1.95

Buy them at your local bookstores or use this handy coupon for ordering:

Please allow 4 to 5 weeks for delivery. This offer expires 12/78.